Tailgating in T-Town

A Recipe Guide to Crimson Tide Tailgating

compiled by Lucy W. Littleton

OWL BAY Publishers

Owl Bay Publishers
P.O. Box 6461
Montgomery, AL 36106

Copyright©1994 by Owl Bay Publishers

Tailgating in T-Town: A Recipe Guide to Crimson Tide Tailgating

Compiled by Lucy W. Littleton
Foreword by Willie Morris
Cover Illustration by Dick Millman
Interior Illustrations by Dorothy Wells
Design, Production, and Copyediting by Word's Worth, Auburn, AL

ISBN 0-9638568-4-7

Manufactured in the United States of America

Table of Contents

Melba Toast
Pita Chips

Finger Food – 30

Buffalo Wings
Spinach Squares
Artichoke Squares
Onion Hors d'Oeuvres
Pepper Jelly Tarts
Pepper Jelly
Smoked Oyster Puffs
Brie Crisps
Krispie Cheese Wafer
Seafood Antipasto
Stuffed Cherry Tomatoes
Stuffed Snow Pea Pods

Stuffed Eggs – 36

Chutney-Stuffed Eggs
Curried Stuffed Eggs
Deviled Eggs with Asparagus Tips
Tuna-Stuffed Eggs
Deviled Eggs & Ham
Deviled Eggs with Crabmeat

Quiche – 39

Salmon Quiche
Zucchini Bacon Mini Quiches
Basic Quiche
Crabmeat Quiche
Stilton Cheese Tart
Leek & Ham Pie
Vidalia Onion Quiche

Bleu Cheese Sandwich Spread
Georgia Peach Sandwiches
Vegetable Sandwiches
Open-Faced Tomato and Cucumber Sandwiches
Roast Beef & French Bread Sandwiches
Sour Cream Biscuits
Traditional Cornish Pasty
Pasties

Salads—page 71

Layered Potato Salad
Sour Cream Potato Salad
Potato Salad Mold
Lettuce & Stilton Salad
Salade Niçoise
Cold Curried Potatoes
Bite-Size Potato Salad
Vidalia Cole Slaw
Creamy Cole Slaw
Slaw
Fruit in Melon Baskets
Pasta Pesto Salad
Pesto Sauce
Rice Salad
Paella Rice Salad
Cold Vegetable Salad
Tabbuli
Steamed Asparagus with Lemon Sauce
Fresh Asparagus Spears
Tomato & Basil or Chervil Salad
Broccoli Salad
Turkey & Fruit Salad
Sheila's Winter Crunch
Steak Salad
Florida Orange Salad with Spinach
Mushroom Chicken Salad
Basic Chicken Salad
Curried Chicken Salad
Chutney Chicken Salad
Imagination Layered Salad

On the Grill—page 91

Kelly Mosley's Pineland Smoked Ham
Grilled Spareribs
Baby Back Ribs
Orange Spareribs
Pork Barbeque
Dr. Wells' Marinade
Smoked Turkey
Barbequed Chicken
Bleu Cheese Burgers
Tallahassee Baked Beans
Marinated Vegetable Kabobs
Lemon Butter Sauce
Grilled Corn on the Cob

Smoked Fish – 99

Smoked Fish
Smoked Mullet
Smoked Butterfly Shrimp

Grilled Seafood – 101

Oyster Roast
Grilled Bream
Grilled Salmon
Salmon Fillets
Tuna or Salmon Steaks
Zesty Shrimp
Backyard Scallops
Spiny Lobster Tails

Kabobs – 104

Dowe's Grilled Shrimp Kabobs
Elizabeth's Shrimp on the Grill
Barbequed Shrimp
Smoky Oyster Kabobs
Franklin's Chicken or Steak Kabobs
Margarita Pork Kabobs
Chicken Wings
Cold Bacon-Wrapped Chicken

Cold Poached Salmon with Cucumber Sauce

Desserts—page 111

Original Nestle Tollhouse Cookies
Butterscotch Icebox Cookies
Nola's Ole Miss Gingersnaps
Peanut Butter Cookies
Butterscotch Brownies
Chocolate Marshmallow Brownies
Never Fail Chewy Brownies
Reese's Cup Cookies
Strawberry Tarts
Lemon Tarts
Cherry Tarts
Pecan Tarts
Miniature Cheesecakes
Chocolate Chip Pecan Pie
Carole's Quick Pecan Pie
Graham Cracker Pralines
Peach Bread Pudding
American Flag Cake

Menus—123

French Picnic
English Picnic
Vegetarian Picnic
Games Away: Listening to the Game on a Boat
Spring Practice: May Wine Brunch
Summer Football Talk: Fourth of July Picnic
New Year's Day Bowl Game: All-Day Picnic

Foreword

by Willie Morris

"In New England, college football is a cultural exercise," the fabled coach Marino Cassem, once known as the Black Godfather of Mississippi, judged some years ago, "on the West Coast it is a tourist attraction, in the Midwest it is cannibalism, but in the South it is religion, and Saturday is the holy day."

College football in the South has forever been an unerring metaphor for the violent and flamboyant and vivid lineaments of its land and legacy, and there is indeed a most vivid religiosity to its vast and complex Saturday tableaux. The tough, hulking linemen often appear worshipful, the big malevolent linebackers seem long since to have committed their enduring souls, and the dexterous running backs are plainly at play in the fields of the Lord. These ineluctable realities carry into the social milieu as well.

In temper with this ambiance of Christian retribution, there is a bloodletting fanaticism to our contretemps, especially, of course, the torrid and most internecine arch-rivalries. I recently attended an Alabama–Auburn match in Birmingham. This, I shall testify for the discriminating and fastidious reader, was *serious* business. Those cerebral heathen of all stripes who reason that Southern football is merely one more sporting event would best come to a Crimson Tide–Tiger game, for life itself seems to hang therein in its balance. After this particular game, a 'Bama man and an Auburn woman were having at it in a hotel lobby in tongue as graphic and dismembering as the Old Testament itself, and as benevolent as Ecclesiastes, I found myself—the outlander—nobly stepping between them, risking Quaker-like one's own bodily vulnerability in the cause of pacifism in the great state of Alabama.

No scholar of the Dixie gridiron can pass his years in this mortal coil without witnessing a night game in Tiger Stadium in Baton Rouge. The sinking sun casts death-like shadows upon this terrain of old tumult, and minutes before kickoff the ceaseless mounting clamor rises in synesthesia, as if a deep blazing crimson, making one feel he is in the presence of some elemental phenomenon of near geologic propensity. Over in the end zone, LSU partisans in an upper deck will likely be pouring beer and whiskey on the visitors' marching band seated below. There is a catharsis descending here, and the accumulating din has often been heard as far away as Cincinnati.

Once at a North Carolina–North Carolina State game in Chapel Hill, in the lovely Kenan Stadium surrounded in its subtle wispy pines, which, as legend has it, the benefactor William Rand Kenan stipulated in 1927 that the height of the stadium never surpass the tallest pine, I was somewhat surprised by the same unruly and soul-baring partisanship, for Chapel Hill by all deserved reputation is a faubourg of much civility, the secluded and bucolic beauty of its campus as recorded by Thomas Wolfe in *Look Homeward, Angel*: "it seemed to Eugene like a provincial outpost of great Rome; one felt its remoteness, its isolated charm." Why, then, was I for this briefest instant unsettled by the clamorous and resolute mass of fidelities? This was the South, wasn't it?

Any student of the Southland's collegiate locales would be advised to sit in the south end zone on a golden, luminous autumn's afternoon at Vaught–Hemingway stadium in Oxford, Mississippi. For some years now a most distinctive cadre of Ole Miss Rebel obstinates have banded together in a roiling section of seats not far behind the goalposts. They call themselves "The South End Zone Bleacher Bums," and their cacophonous interracial number include William Faulkner's niece, famous novelists, eminent historians, black bartenders, wealthy landscape painters, museum curators, literary archivists, female mayors, and also an occasional vagrant mountebank or charlatan. They, too, are noisome, as when coach "Dog" Brewer strolled their way in pre-games to observe his behemoth linemen at their starkest calisthenics near the end zone: "*Dog! Dog! Dog!*," and he would wriggle a finger their way in private recognition of his perfervid aficionados. When the half black, half white Rebel offense is marching toward this especial goal line, a beloved woman of this regiment unravels a large hand-painted sign she always brings and drapes it over the field-level rampart: "Come to Us, Our Lovelies!" When Vanderbilt is in pilgrimage from Nashville: "Trounce the Eggheads!" or "Down with the Existentialists!"

I have gone to college matches down here since age seven, when my father took me to my first one in a torrential rainstorm at old Crump Field in Memphis involving the Razorbacks of Arkansas and the Rebels of Ole Miss and even as a grown man am absorbed with the rituals and nuances and whims and catastrophes of the Southern game. These scenes return to me now in widening montage: the phantasmagoric marching bands of the black universities of the Southwest Athletic Conference, whose dexterous expertise and showmanship are rightful legend, particularly the Sonic Boom of Jackson State; the deepening shadows upon a close and fluttery contest in the fourth quarters Between the Hedges at Athens, when a bizarre silence falls, and man's fate itself appears at issue and suspended; a storm of near hurricane dimensions at an Independence Bowl in Shreveport when a sky-diving team descends before the coin toss toward the turf in the thunder and lightning, one of their number culminating on the Coliseum roof a quarter of a mile away; Death Valley at Clemson, rivalling Auburn's Jordan–Hare and Tiger Stadium of LSU in its noise quotient; the broiling heat of September and early October in the home fields of the Old Confederacy when even the most intrepid visiting Yankee squads will sometimes wilt and dissolve; Bryant–Denny Stadium in Tuscaloosa with the heavenly ecclesiastic aura of the Bear in this Vatican City of Football; skeletal Doak Campbell Stadium in moss-draped Tallahassee. And on and on.

And over all of this, in my recollections, linger the hovering spirit of time passing, of old classic clashes revered and remembered, of beautiful willowy long-ago cheerleaders and lithesome majorettes now in the Great Gridiron in the Sky, of mythic eighty-yard runs and immemorial goal-line stands. For as with most other things in this Southland, its violent encompassing football dwells forever in the sinew and fabric and deep heart's blood of its sorrow and complexity and remembrance.

Consistent with all this, the tailgating at Southern college games are a subculture all their own, for the social territory itself envelopes and elicits this most indigenous spirituality and color and mayhem. At these tailgatings, the women are more stylishly dressed than at parallel American venues. At a Notre Dame–Ole Miss game I witnessed in South Bend a few years ago, someone observed: "The only women in this stadium in fur coats are from Mississippi."

Among other things, there is more drinking at these Dixie gridiron tailgatings, I peremptorily venture to assess, than at their sociological counterparts in all other provinces of the Great Republic. The drinking begins early and lasts late and is imbued with the profound bilious heritage. In many of the stadia, attendants are on guard at the entry gates to detect the surreptitious pints and fifths, more often than not to inefficious avail. Wives and girlfriends are known to sneak through the booze in substantial mouthwash containers in their purses (Has anyone noticed that Listerine bears a sly resemblance to sour mash whiskey?), and one of the large sellers in gift stores down here in the autumns are hollow ersatz binoculars with flasks concealed inside.

Of the Southern tailgatings I have personally witnessed, the ones outside Tiger Stadium in Baton Rouge are in all aspects legendary. Many of the LSU loyalists from the bayous and canebrakes of this bizarre and notable state gather upon this gregarious setting considerably before twilight on Friday and continue their raucous celebration until the Saturday night kickoff. Here they drink like Russians. In addition to the usual accoutrements, crawfish étouffée is more often than not a principal course, not to mention the gumbo, of course. LSU fans, as I have previously suggested, have a reputation for a certain unhesitant belligerence toward football visitors, but even as an Ole Miss advocate in this singular and long-standing rivalry walking toward the stadium for the game I have been hospitably invited by Bayou Bengal gourmands to sit with them and sample the pungent Cajun delicacies, "We're gonna whip your ___'s," one says, "but have a little étouffée first." At an Alabama–Auburn game I attended in Birmingham, a number of sizable tents had been pitched outside Legion Field with lengthy bars and buffet tables, and the Crimson Tide and Tiger zealots eyed one another with uneasy and most ambivalent tolerance across a strip of neutral ground with all the appearance of a DMZ. Occasionally, a few of the rivals who must have known each other from church or the workplace emerged from the respective tents to say hello, but when they left for the kickoff I was reminded from my readings of the Northern and Southern cadets at West Point in 1860 departing their separate ways to go at one another in the Civil War to come. . . . Few more pristine spots of tailgating can be found than at the Tennessee games in Knoxville, where not far from the second largest college stadium in the country (next to Ann Arbor) many of the Volunteer revelers have their parties on boats anchored in the Tennessee River. . . . At a Georgia–Florida weekend in Jacksonville some time back, I finally bore eternal witness to the World's Largest Outdoor Cocktail Party, which in its sweep and verve exceeded all existential expectation, resembling for me nothing if not New Year's Eve on Times Square in Manhattan, but lasting longer and covering considerably more acreage and with more tangible passion per capita than any of the orgies Gibbon wrote about in *The Rise and Fall of the Roman Empire*. And what, pray, did the decadent Romans know of the shovel pass?

The tailgatings I know far more intimately than all others, however, are the ones at Ole Miss in Oxford, where for several years in the 1980s I was the writer-in-residence, and to which, for better or worse, I have invested considerable emotion.

First, I must set the scene, physical and historic, for it is of a piece with the partying. There is a palpable, affecting sophistication to this stunningly beautiful campus in the midst of the rolling rural woodlands of the American South. In the juxtaposition of town and school, many have been reminded of the Chapel Hill of a generation or two ago, which bustles so now within the perimeters of the Research Triangle.

Foremost all around the little town and campus are the Faulknerian landmarks. Beginning at the courthouse square with its Confederate soldier facing southward and the benches on the lawn crowded with sunburnt men chewing tobacco, one will follow the shady, settled streets with the antebellum houses hidden in magnolias or crepe myrtles. Their names are Shadow Lawn, Rowan Oak, Memory House. One may stroll by the oldest domicile in town, which was built in 1830. In front of the jail, aged white and black men wearing Ole Miss baseball caps sit in haphazard conversation. The Ole Miss students speed by in their cars, their mindless shouts and laughter trailing behind them, and there will be dusty pickups with farmers in khakis from Beat Four. The sorority girls have been in their rooms on campus painting their toenails, when one of them shouts: "Anybody want to go buy some *shoes*?" Everything is a blend of the town and the enveloping, untouched country.

The campus will be only a few blocks down University Avenue from the courthouse square. Here the town and the university come together. In the bowers and groves lush with dogwood and forsythia in the spring and blazing with color in the fall, students sit together under the trees, or drift languidly toward their classrooms. The old Lyceum is at the crest of the hill, and the library with its inscription: "I believe that man will not merely endure . . . he will prevail." Not far from here is the football stadium, where 40,000 souls—four times more than the population of the town—will unquietly congregate on the poignant autumnal afternoons.

Ole Miss is a place of ghosts. Almost no other American campus envelops deaths and suffering and blood, and the fire and sword, as Ole Miss does. In the American Civil War, it was closed down and became a hospital for both sides. The bloodbath of Shiloh was only eighty miles away. Hundreds of boys on both sides died on the campus, their corpses stacked like cordwood, buried now in unmarked graves in a nearby glade. There is a Confederate statue on the campus also, given to the university by the Faulkners as the one on the courthouse square was.

The conjunction of all this is the Ole Miss Grove, a large and felicitous apex in the center of the campus shaded by its towering old oaks and elms and gums and hollies with their rhapsodic autumn foliage. The Saturday football context is a vibrant one, for the imbibing for many has begun not long after dawn, thousands of Rebel celebrants, many of their number aggregating around tables arranged with fine china on linen tablecloths, and silver candelabra and football helmets garnished with natural flowers. Affectionate Mississippi salutations echo across this timeless terrain, and the socializing is—shall one say—somewhat intense. The game on this day in the toughest and most unrelenting of American football conferences will be with Alabama, or Auburn, or Arkansas, or Florida, or Georgia, or Tennessee, or the notorious football factory Vanderbilt, in the perfect little stadium down the way with its resonances of Bruiser Kennard, and Archie Manning, and Jake Gibbs, and Squirrel Griffing, and Gentle Ben Williams, and Buford McGee, and little boys of all ages and races in miniature Ole Miss jerseys toss footballs among the tables, and little girls in Rebel cheerleaders' suits rehearse their "Hotty Toddies." Soon the football team itself will stroll through this exuberant throng in single-file to the stadium, the Rebel warriors with game faces resolutely set, and the accolades as they progress down the Grove roll across this warm-blooded site in mounting rivulet and crescendo. Soon the ballplayers disappear among the young magnolias abutting the locker room, and the partying resumes anew. Of course it will. It's indeed the South, isn't it?

Beverages
and
Hors d'Oeuvres

Beverages

Bloody Marie for 6

3 cups tomato juice
2½ cups Sauterne
⅓ cup lemon juice

Combine and serve over ice.

Bloody Mary

four 46-oz. cans V8 juice
1 qt. Vodka
6-oz. bottle of Worcestershire
2 lemons, juice only
1 tsp. celery salt
Tabasco to taste

Mix together and chill. Makes 36 Bloody Marys.

May Wine

2 cups sliced strawberries
2 tbsp. sugar
2 qts. Sauterne or Rhine wine
1 bottle chilled champagne

Sprinkle strawberries with sugar. Add Sauterne and allow to steep overnight or at least four hours. Strain out fruit. At serving time, pour over ice ring in punch bowl and pour in champagne. Serve in wine glasses. Serves 6.

Line a large wicker basket with plastic and aluminum foil, fill it with ice and bottles of wine, decorate with bunches of green and purple grapes.

Frozen Strawberry Daiquiris

3 boxes frozen strawberries, or 3 boxes fresh
  strawberries, washed, hulled, and mashed
6-oz. can frozen limeade
6-oz. can frozen lemonade
½ cup grenadine
⅘ cup light rum
water

Blend all ingredients, adding enough water to make 1 gallon. Freeze.
Store only a short time.

Frozen Daiquiri

6-oz. can frozen limeade
three 6-oz. cans frozen lemonade
8 cups water
1 fifth light rum or vodka

Mix and pour into plastic containers and freeze. The alcohol will prevent a
hard freeze. Ready to serve.

Frozen Daiquiris with Sprite

2 sm. limes, juice only
1 lemon, juice only
3 cans water
24 oz. Sprite
1 fifth of rum

Combine ingredients in large plastic container and freeze. When preparing
drink, half mixture & half Sprite.

Sangria Blanc

2 bottles dry white wine
1/2 cup sugar
1 cup triple sec
1 cup vodka
1 qt. bottle club soda
1 orange, 2 lemons, 1 lime

Place fruit (sliced thinly with seeds removed) and triple sec in glass jar and refrigerate along with wine and club soda overnight. In serving container mix sugar with wine and stir until dissolved. Stir in rest of ingredients and serve over lemonade ice ring or ice cubes made out of lemonade.

Frozen Margarita

10-oz. can Bacardi frozen Margarita Mix
1 can rum or tequila
two 10-oz. cans water

Stir to mix. Freeze in covered plastic container and carry to picnic surrounded by ice. If it melts, serve over ice.

Lemonade Iced Tea

3 qts. tea
12-oz. can frozen lemonade
1 bottle ginger ale

Make tea and stir in lemonade. Just before serving add ginger ale and serve over crushed ice. This is nice garnished with mint that can be carried in a zip lock bag. Also you might want to carry sugar cubes for those who like sweeter tea.

Mint Tea

4 tea bags
1 bunch of fresh mint leaves
½ cup sugar
the juice of two lemons or limes

Put tea bags and fresh mint into a teapot or Pyrex 2-qt. measuring cup. Pour 3 cups of boiling water over this. Let stand about 5 minutes and strain into a pitcher with sugar. Stir to dissolve. Cool tea and add lemon or lime juice. Serve over ice. If your friends don't all like sugar in their tea, leave out sugar and carry sugar lumps.

Toomer's Corner Lemonade

5 pounds sugar
1 pint of lemon juice

Make 1 gallon of simple syrup as follows: Put sugar in a gallon jug and fill the jug with water. Stir or shake until sugar dissolves and solution is clear. (Hot water makes the sugar dissolve more quickly.) To make one gallon of lemonade, pour 1 pint of lemon juice and 2 pints of simple syrup in a gallon container. At serving time fill gallon jar with crushed ice and water. Stir and serve.

Lemonade

3 lemons squeezed—save rinds
1 cup sugar
2 qts. boiling water

Squeeze lemons and pound skins in large bowl. Add sugar and stir. Pour in boiling water and stir until sugar is dissolved. Cool. Remove lemon rinds and carry in Thermos. Serve over ice.

Hors d'Oeuvres

Dips and Spreads

Dips may be taken in covered plastic containers and either served from them, or in a hollowed out cabbage or other vegetable (eggplant or pepper) or in a hollowed out round loaf of bread. A seafood dip is pretty served from a large sea shell. Transport in a cooler in a covered container that can double as a serving dish.

New Years Day
Black-Eyed Pea Dip

15½-oz. can black-eyed peas, drained & slightly
   mashed
1 lb. ground sausage
1 lb. Velveeta cheese, cut into cubes
10-oz. can Rotel tomatoes
¼ cup chopped onion

In large frying pan, cook sausage and onion until done. Drain grease and add tomatoes and drained peas. Simmer 20 minutes. Stir in cheese until it all melts. Add salt and pepper to taste. Serve with corn chips.

Eggplant Dip

1 med. eggplant
¼ cup chopped onion
½ cup milk
1 tbsp. oil
1 lemon, juice only
1 tbsp. oleo
1 tbsp. flour
3 oz. Parmesan cheese
salt, pepper, nutmeg

Prick eggplant with a fork, rub with oil and bake uncovered in 400-degree oven for 1 hour or until pulp is soft. Scoop out pulp into saucepan, add lemon juice and cook over medium heat until liquid has evaporated. In another saucepan, melt butter, sauté onion and blend in flour. Add milk and cook until smooth white sauce. Fold white sauce into eggplant and add other ingredients. Thin with milk if necessary. Store overnight before serving at room temperature with crackers. Freezes well.

Guacamole Dip

2 lg. ripe avocadoes, peeled and chopped
6 green onions, with part of green chopped off
4-oz. can chili peppers, chopped (optional)
½ lemon, juice only
salt & pepper
1 tomato, chopped

In processor purée avocados. Stir in other ingredients except tomatoes. Put avocado pit in guacamole and chill in plastic covered container. At serving time, stir in tomato and serve with corn chips. If you don't use peppers, flavor with a few drops of Tabasco sauce.

Mexico Olé Dip

16-oz. can refried beans
10½-oz. can bean dip
2 tbsp. jalapeño peppers
10 oz. Monterey Jack cheese, grated
10 oz. sharp cheddar cheese, grated
2 cups sour cream
1 package taco seasoning
8-oz. bottle Picante sauce
guacamole spread (or 2 ripe avocados)
1 lemon, juice only
1 sm. onion, finely chopped
2 tomatoes, finely chopped
4.2-oz. can sliced olives, drained

In a 2-qt. oblong casserole, spread a mixture of refried beans, bean dip, and jalapeño peppers. Sprinkle on Monterey Jack, then cheddar cheese. Mix sour cream and taco seasoning; smooth on top of cheese. Pour Picante sauce over all. At serving time, add a layer of guacamole sauce, onions, tomatoes, and black olives in that order. Serve with pita chips.

Onion Mums: Peel a white onion. Cutting only to ½" from bottom, slice down center; cut into quarters; cut quarters into eighths. If you wish a fuller flower, place toothpicks between radial cuts to hold blossom open. Remove toothpicks before serving. Use to center crudités plates.

Curry Dip

1¾ cup mayonnaise
2 tbsp. catsup
2 tbsp. honey
4 tbsp. grated onion
1 tbsp. lemon juice
Tabasco to taste
1 tsp. curry powder

Combine and refrigerate until ready to serve. Wonderful with fresh vegetables.

Boursin Cheese

8 oz. cream cheese, softened
1 clove garlic, crushed
2 tsp. freshly minced parsley
½ tsp. basil leaves
2 tbsp. chopped chives
1 tbsp. dry white vermouth or wine
Pinch of hot pepper sauce

Blend cream cheese with garlic. Add remaining ingredients. Chill. To make a dip, add ½ cup sour cream. Make before leaving for picnic.

All of these cheese spreads are good stuffed in celery sticks.

Beer Cheese

1 lb. sharp cheddar
1 lb. Swiss cheese
1 tsp. dry mustard
⅛ tsp. garlic powder
1 tsp. Worcestershire
1 cup beer

Shred cheese and blend with other ingredients. Age 6 days. Serve room temperature.

Roquefort Cheese Ball

16 oz. cream cheese
8 oz. roquefort cheese
½ cup mayonnaise
4 tsp. lemon juice
1 garlic bud, pressed
1 sm. onion, grated
¼ tsp. Tabasco
caviar (to be placed in hollow center)

Mix cheeses at room temperature. Add mayonnaise. Add remaining ingredients and blend well. Form a deep hollow on top and put caviar in center. (Rinse the caviar in a strainer and carry separately to the picnic and put on the cheese ball at the last minute.) Serve with plain or Melba toast.

Pineapple Cheese Ball

two 8-oz. packages cream cheese, softened
8¼-oz. can crushed pineapple
2 cups chopped pecans
¼ cup finely chopped bell pepper
2 tbsp. finely chopped onion
1 tbsp. Lawry's seasoned salt

In medium bowl mix cream cheese until smooth. Gradually stir in pineapple, 1 cup pecans, pepper, onion & salt. Shape into ball. Roll the ball in remaining nuts, wrap in plastic wrap and refrigerate until chilled. Serves 20.

Shrimp or Tuna Paté

10-oz. can tuna, drained
1 cup butter, softened and cut into pieces
½ tsp. lemon juice
few shakes Tabasco
salt & pepper
3 tbsp. capers, drained
Melba toast
parsley

Place tuna, butter, juice, Tabasco, salt & pepper in food processor; process until thoroughly mixed; add capers. Process until combined. Spoon into an oiled mold and chill overnight. Unmold and garnish with parsley. Serve with Melba toast. Can be frozen, then thawed for several hours on the way to the game. To make shrimp paté, you may substitute an equal amount of finely chopped cooked shrimp or washed & well-drained canned shrimp doctored up with lemon juice and Tabasco.

Smoked Fish Paté

1 lb. smoked mullet (or other smoked fish)
two 8-oz. packages cream cheese, softened
3 tbsp. lemon juice
½ tsp. Worcestershire sauce
few shakes Tabasco
2 tbsp. grated onion
3 tbsp. chopped parsley
assorted crackers

Garnish:
parsley sprigs

Remove skin and bones from fish. Flake the fish. Combine cream cheese, lemon juice, and grated onion and whip until smooth and fluffy. Stir in fish and chopped parsley. Chill for one hour. Garnish with parsley. Serve with crackers. Makes about 3½ cups of spread.

Smoked Salmon Ball

1 lb. smoked salmon, drained, boned, skinned
8-oz. package of cream cheese, softened
1 tbsp. lemon juice
2 tsp. grated onion
1 tsp. horseradish

Garnish:
chopped parsley
chopped pecans

Blend ingredients and form into log. Chill in plastic wrap several hours or overnight. Before serving coat with chopped parsley and finely chopped pecans. Serves 24. Leftovers may be frozen. A 15½-oz. can of red salmon may be substituted for the smoked salmon. Add ¼ tsp. liquid smoke to the recipe if you make this substitution.

Oyster Roll

two 8-oz. packages cream cheese
1 can smoked oysters, drained and chopped
1 clove garlic, pressed
2 tbsp. Worcestershire
dash Tabasco
2-3 tbsp. mayonnaise
½ sm. onion, grated

Combine all ingredients except smoked oysters. Blend with fork until smooth. Spread into a rectangle about ½" thick on waxed paper. Sprinkle chopped oysters over top of cheese and roll like a jelly roll, starting off cheese, with a spatula edge. Chill 24 hours. Serve with Melba toast.

Potted Shrimp

2 cups deveined shelled, cooked tiny shrimp
½ cup lemon juice
1 cup softened unsalted sweet butter
2 tbsp. snipped fresh dill
2 tsp. minced anchovy fillets
¼ tsp. salt
pinch Cayenne pepper
1 tbsp. coarsely ground black pepper
dill sprig

Combine shrimp and lemon juice in small bowl. Let stand covered at room temperature 1 hour. Drain. Cream butter in large mixer bowl. Beat in dill, anchovies, salt and cayenne pepper. Fold in shrimp, taste, and adjust seasonings. Spoon shrimp mixture into small earthenware crock. Sprinkle top with black pepper. Refrigerate overnight. Serve on crackers at room temperature; garnish with dill.

Potted Smoked Trout or Salmon

8 oz. smoked trout or salmon
1 tsp. horseradish
2 tbsp. softened butter
4 oz. cream cheese
2 tbsp. sour cream
1 tbsp. lemon juice
½ tsp. mace
salt & pepper

Purée trout or salmon with horseradish in food processor. Add rest of ingredients to processor and blend until smooth. Put in custard cups or ceramic pot and top with clarified butter. Serve at room temperature on whole wheat Melba toast. Serves 8.

Tuna Mold

2 cans tuna, drained
1 can tomato soup
1½ packages unflavored gelatin
8-oz. package cream cheese
½ cup each finely chopped celery, onion and green
    pepper
1 cup Durkee's dressing
1 sm. bottle black or green olives

Heat soup and melt cream cheese in it. Smooth with hand mixer. Dissolve gelatin in soup and cool. Chop olives and flake tuna and add it to soup mixture along with other ingredients. Mix well. Pour into plastic wrap-lined fish mold and chill. Cover with more plastic wrap. Carry in cooler. At picnic site, unmold. Use on crackers or as a salad. Shrimp or salmon may be substituted for tuna.

Any cream cheese recipe can be made lighter by substituting Neufchâtel for cream cheese.

Chicken Paté

3½ lb. chicken breasts & thighs
2 med. onions, diced
2 tbsp. butter
3 eggs
2 tbsp. mustard
1 lemon (juice)
2 cloves garlic, pressed
8 oz. whipping cream
salt
1 tsp. thyme
1 tsp. hot pepper sauce

Bake chicken 40 minutes in 400 degree oven. Sauté onions in butter. Skin and bone chicken and food process. Add other ingredients and process until smooth. Pour into greased bread loaf pan and put in pan filled half way with water. Bake at 375 degrees until firm (about 1 hour). Cool, chill in fridge. Garnish with fresh thyme. (This is very mild. If you like spicy food you may want to add more flavoring and herbs.)

Chicken Liver Paté

1 lb. chicken livers
1 onion, chopped
2 cloves garlic, pressed
1 stick real butter
salt & pepper
pinch of dried thyme
1 tbsp. brandy or wine

Melt 2 tbsp. butter and sauté garlic and onion until soft. Remove from pan and sauté livers about 5 minutes, adding more butter if necessary. Cool. Purée in food processor. Cream butter and beat into livers. Season to taste. Chill and mold. Serve with brown bread.

Mushroom & Chicken Paté

¾ cup butter or margarine
½ lb. fresh mushrooms, sliced
1 lb. chicken livers
1 tsp. garlic salt
⅓ cup green onions, finely chopped
½ cup white table wine
3 drops bottled red pepper sauce
1 tsp. salt

Garnish:
parsley
lemon slices

Melt ¼ cup butter or margarine in skillet. Add mushrooms, livers, garlic salt, and onions; simmer for 5 minutes. Add wine and pepper sauce; cover and cook slowly for 5 to 10 minutes longer. Cool; whirl in blender, adding remaining ½ cup butter (softened) and salt to taste. Turn into dish; chill overnight. Unmold; garnish with parsley and thin lemon slices. Makes 3 cups.

All patés and spreads are good on Melba toast.

Melba Toast

Cut crust from very thin slices of bread. Cut into desired shapes. Place on cookie sheet and toast in slow oven until crisp and slightly browned, about 20 minutes. Brush with butter and sprinkle with paprika, if desired.

Pita Chips

Separate pita into two rounds, then cut into wedges. Brush lightly with melted butter. Place on baking sheet and bake at 400 degrees until lightly browned (about 7 to 8 minutes).

Finger Food

Buffalo Wings

2½ lbs. chicken wings
½ cup butter or margarine, melted
¼ cup hot sauce
tomato paste

Split wings at each joint and pat dry. Melt butter in baking dish and bake wings at 400 degrees for 1 hour, turning halfway through. Thicken hot sauce with enough tomato paste to stick to wings. Shake few at a time in covered container with sauce until coated. Serves 8.

Spinach Squares

two 10-oz. packages frozen, chopped spinach
3 tbsp. butter
1 med. onion, chopped
¼ lb. mushrooms, sliced
4 eggs, beaten
¼ cup fine bread crumbs
1 can cream of mushroom soup
¼ cup grated Parmesan cheese
⅛ tsp. pepper
⅛ tsp. oregano
⅛ tsp. basil

Thaw spinach and press out water. Melt butter in frying pan and sauté onion and mushrooms. Combine eggs, bread crumbs, mushroom soup, 2 tbsp. cheese, seasonings, and spinach. Blend with onion mixture. Turn into greased 9" square pan and sprinkle with remaining cheese. Bake uncovered at 325 degrees for 35 minutes. Cool slightly and refrigerate. Cut into 1" squares and serve.

Artichoke Squares

14-oz. can artichoke hearts, drained
½ lb. sharp cheese, grated
1 green onion, chopped
4 eggs
6 saltine crackers, crushed
Tabasco to taste
salt & pepper

Chop artichoke hearts into small pieces. Sauté chopped onion in small amount of oil. Beat eggs. Put onion with other ingredients in bowl and mix. Pour mixture into greased 9" square pan and bake at 350 degrees for 20-30 minutes until firm. Cut into tiny pieces and serve hot or cold. This can also be used as a vegetable cut into serving size squares. Cook in Pyrex, Corning, or glass pan.

Onion Hors d'Oeuvres

8-oz. package cream cheese
1 cup mayonnaise
½ cup finely chopped onions
¼ cup Parmesan cheese
sm. can of shrimp, drained

Combine all but shrimp, spread on bread rounds, top with shrimp, and sprinkle with paprika. Bake at 350 degrees until puffy. This is great even without shrimp or onion.

Use Onion hors d'Oeuvres only if you have an R.V. or houseboat with a stove, because they're only good hot.

Pepper Jelly Tarts

3-oz. package cream cheese, softened
1 stick butter
1 cup flour, sifted
⅛ tsp. salt
pepper jelly (recipe follows)

Mix cream cheese and butter until smooth. Add flour and salt gradually until well blended. Make into ball and refrigerate until well chilled. Roll out dough and cut into circles with wine glass. Put 1 teaspoon pepper jelly on each circle and fold in half. Seal edges and bake at 400 degrees for 10 minutes.

Pepper Jelly

12 green peppers
1 med. hot green pepper
7 cups granulated sugar
1 tsp. turmeric
1 1/2 cup cider vinegar
6-oz. bottle liquid fruit pectin
green food coloring (optional)

Cut peppers in half, remove stem and seeds and put peppers through food processor or blender. Chop fine. Drain well and measure 2 cups green pepper into large saucepan. Add sugar, vinegar, turmeric. Mix well. Place over high heat, bring to a full rolling boil and let it boil hard for 1 minute, stirring constantly. Remove from heat and stir in pectin immediately. Stir and skim off foam for 5 minutes. Add a little food coloring, if desired, and mix well. Ladle quickly into hot, sterilized glasses. Pour melted paraffin over top to seal. Makes about ten 6-oz. glasses.

Smoked Oyster Puffs

1/2 lb. oleo or butter, softened
8 oz. cream cheese, softened
2 cups all-purpose flour
1 can smoked oysters or anchovy paste

Cream together oleo and cheese. Stir in flour. Chill. Roll thin and cut with small biscuit cutter. Place piece of smoked oyster, or else spread anchovy paste, in middle of dough. Fold in half, press edges of dough together and bake at 450 degrees for 10 minutes.

For this and the pepper jelly turnovers, pie crust mix fixed according to directions works very well.

Brie Crisps

4 oz. Brie cheese, room temperature
½ cup (1 stick) butter, room temperature
⅔ cup all-purpose flour
2 dashes hot pepper sauce
paprika

Combine cheese and butter in processor and mix until creamy. Add flour, pepper sauce, and salt and mix, using on/off turns, until dough almost forms ball. Turn dough out onto large piece of plastic wrap and shape into loose cylinder 2 inches in diameter. Wrap dough tightly in plastic and refrigerate for 30 minutes. Roll dough into smooth even cylinder about 1½ inches in diameter and 8 inches long. Rewrap dough in plastic and refrigerate overnight. Preheat oven to 325 degrees. Slice cylinder into ¼"-thick rounds. Sprinkle with paprika. Arrange on baking sheet, spacing about 2 inches. Bake at 325 degrees until done (about 10-12 minutes). Don't overcook. Makes 3 dozen.

Krispie Cheese Wafers

2 sticks oleo
2 cups sharp cheddar, grated
2 cups flour
½ tsp. salt
¼ tsp. hot pepper sauce
2 cups Rice Krispies

Mix oleo and cheese well. Add salt, cayenne pepper, and flour. Add 2 cups Rice Krispies, folding in by hand. Form into small balls, place on ungreased baking sheet. Mash flat with back of fork. Bake at 325 degrees for 15 minutes or more, until firm.

Seafood Antipasto

1 lb. scallops
7 tbsp. olive oil
2 tsp. lemon juice
1 lb. shrimp, cubed
1 tbsp. dry minced onion
1 tbsp. sugar
1 tsp. salt
½ tsp. garlic powder
½ tsp. black pepper
½ tsp. red pepper
¼ cup fresh basil leaves, or less to taste
6-oz. can sm. ripe olives
1 jar green olives
4½-oz. can whole mushrooms
8½-oz. can artichoke hearts, drained
12 oz. white cheddar
1 cup vegetable oil
⅔ cup vinegar

Cook scallops in 4 tbsp. olive oil over high heat 2 to 4 minutes until opaque. Remove and stir in lemon juice. Do the same with 3 tbsp. oil and shrimp. Combine sugar and spices. In 9"x13" dish, arrange ⅛ cup basil, sprinkle ½ spice mixture. Add seafood, etc. and top with basil/sugar. Combine oil and vinegar. Pour over seafood marinade overnight.

Stuffed Cherry Tomatoes

cherry tomatoes
your choice of filling

Cut tops off tomatoes and scoop out pulp and seeds with ½ tsp. measuring spoon or melon baller. (You may freeze this tomato for later use in soups or chili.) Turn tomatoes upside down and drain on dish towel for a few hours. Fill with vegetable sandwich mix, seafood salads, cream cheese mixtures, egg salad or filling of your choice.

Stuffed Snow Pea Pods

Bring water to boil and put pea pods in a steamer basket. Reduce heat and simmer 1 minute. Immediately remove peas and refresh under cold water. Refrigerate until cool. Slit peas down one side and stuff with cream cheese mixture such as Boursin Cheese.

Stuffed Eggs

Chutney-Stuffed Eggs

> 6 hard-boiled eggs
> 3 slices crisp-cooked bacon, crumbled
> 1½ tbsp. mayonnaise
> 3 tbsp. finely chopped chutney
> salt

Halve eggs and remove yolks from egg whites, setting aside the white for stuffing. Combine all ingredients well and fill reserved egg whites.

When transporting Stuffed Eggs, Tupperware makes an excellent stuffed egg keeper with insets holding lengthwise sliced egg halves. If you don't have one, cut the eggs crosswise, stuff, put back together, and carry in egg cartons lined with plastic wrap. Keep eggs in cooler.

Curried Stuffed Eggs

6 hard-boiled eggs
1 tbsp. snipped fresh chives
1 tbsp. soft butter
1 tbsp. mayonnaise
1 tsp. Dijon mustard
2 tsp. curry powder
salt & pepper
chopped chutney

Peel eggs and cut in half lengthwise. Mash yolks in small bowl. Add chives, butter, mayonnaise, and mustard and mix well. Mix in curry powder, according to taste. Season with salt and pepper. Fill egg whites cavities with yolk mixture. Refrigerate. At serving time, garnish the center of each stuffed egg with a dab of chopped chutney.

Deviled Eggs with Asparagus Tips

8 hard-boiled eggs
3 tbsp. mayonnaise
3 tsp. grated lemon rind
1/2 tsp. curry powder
1/4 tsp. dry mustard
16 asparagus tips
salt
dash pepper sauce

Cut eggs lengthwise, scoop out and mash yolks. Add mayonnaise, lemon rind, pepper sauce, salt, curry powder, and mustard. Fill egg whites with mixture. Garnish with asparagus tips.

Tuna-Stuffed Eggs

12 hard-boiled eggs
6½-oz. can of water-packed tuna, drained & rinsed
½ cup minced celery
3 tbsp. minced green pepper
1 tsp. prepared mustard
¼ tsp. salt
6 tbsp. mayonnaise

Mince vegetables very finely. Slice eggs in half and remove yolks. In a small bowl mash yolks and add remaining ingredients. Fill egg whites.

Capers are good added to stuffed eggs.

Deviled Eggs & Ham

6 hard-boiled eggs
3 slices boiled ham
2 tbsp. chopped chives
1 tbsp. Dijon mustard
3 tbsp. mayonnaise
1 tbsp. sour cream
salt & pepper
2 tbsp. fresh lemon thyme leaves (or 2 tsp. dried)

Halve the eggs; place the yolks in a bowl. Mince the ham (potted ham may be substituted for sliced ham). Mash the yolks until very fine. Stir in chives, the minced ham, mustard, mayonnaise, and sour cream. Season with salt & pepper. Fill the whites with the yolk mixture.

Deviled Eggs with Crabmeat

12 hard-boiled eggs
1½ sticks of butter
8 oz. crabmeat
2 tbsp. Parmesan cheese
1 tsp. Dijon mustard
1 clove garlic, pressed
⅛ tsp. Tabasco
1 tsp. each, salt & pepper
1 tsp. lemon juice
2 tsp. tomato paste, optional
1 tbsp. chopped parsley

Peel eggs, halve, and remove yolks. Save egg whites. Place yolks and all other ingredients in a food processor until smooth. Restuff egg whites.

Quiche

Salmon Quiche

1 pastry shell (prebaked at 400 degrees for 8 minutes)
1 cup cooked, flaked salmon
4 tbsp. chopped dill
2 tbsp. chopped parsley
4 eggs
¼ cup half & half or whipping cream
¼ cup grated Parmesan cheese
pepper

Preheat oven to 350 degrees. Put salmon on bottom of pie shell, sprinkle with dill and parsley. Beat eggs, add cream and Parmesan and whisk together. Add pepper and pour into pastry shell. Bake about 40 minutes until custard has set and serve warm or cool.

Quiches may be served hot or at room temperature. To keep them warm wrap in aluminum foil and newspaper. Keep in Styrofoam chest with other hot dishes. Quiches may be carried in their own dishes covered with foil. Cut quiches before leaving home or bake in tart shells. Bring pie server for whole quiches.

Zucchini Bacon Mini Quiches

8 frozen tart shells
2 eggs, beaten
1/2 cup milk
1 3/4 cups zucchini, grated
6 slices bacon, cooked and crumbled
1/2 cup Mozzarella, grated
1/4 tsp. basil
1/4 tsp. oregano
1/4 tsp. hot sauce

Preheat oven to 375 degrees. Prick bottom and sides of frozen tart shells with fork. Bake shells for 5 minutes then remove from oven. Reduce oven temperature to 325 degrees. In medium mixing bowl thoroughly combine remaining ingredients, Spoon mixture into shells; place on cookie sheet and bake for 30 to 40 minutes or until set. Makes 8 mini quiches. (You may make this in 1 deep-dish pie shell.) *From Florida Department of Agriculture and Consumer Services.*

To prebake pie shells for quiche, bake in a 400-degree oven for 5 minutes before filling.

Basic Quiche

2 strips cooked bacon, crumbled
1 cup diced smoked ham
1 cup grated Swiss or cheddar cheese
9" unbaked pie shell (thawed, if frozen)
4 eggs
1½ cups half & half
¼ tsp. ground nutmeg
freshly ground pepper

Preheat oven to 350 degrees. Spread bacon, ham, and cheese inside pie shell. Beat eggs and add half & half, nutmeg, and pepper. Pour over the cheese mixture. Bake about 45 minutes or until the custard is set and the top is lightly browned.

Crabmeat Quiche

10-oz. can lump crabmeat (fresh only)
1 cup coarsely grated Monterey Jack or Swiss
    cheese
3 eggs
1½ cups light cream
¼ cup white wine
2 tsp. salt
½ tsp. pepper
1 pie shell

Prebake pie shell 5 minutes at 400 degrees. Drain crabmeat, picking over well for shells, and toss lightly with cheese. Set aside. Spoon all of combined crabmeat and cheese into the crust. Combine eggs, light cream, wine, salt, and pepper. Beat well. Pour half of custard over crabmeat in pie crust and bake at 325 degrees about 50 minutes or until knife inserted in center of custard comes out clean. *Variation*: To make Avocado–Crabmeat Quiche, use the recipe above, but slice an avocado and arrange in the bottom of the pie shell. Sprinkle avocado with 1 tbsp. lemon juice to keep from darkening, then add crabmeat and cheese mixture, and bake.

Stilton Cheese Tart

3 oz. Stilton (or bleu) cheese, crumbled
6 oz. cream cheese
2 tbsp. butter, softened
¼ cup whipping cream
2 eggs
½ tsp. salt
¼ tsp. pepper
1 tbsp. chopped fresh chives
8" pie shell, partially baked

Prebake pie shell 5 minutes at 400 degrees. Blend cheeses, butter, and cream in food processor. Beat in eggs. Season and stir in chives. Pour into pie shell and bake at 325 degrees for 30 minutes, or until top is light brown and knife comes out clean.

If you want to, you may bake any of these quiches in mini muffin pans, but reduce the cooking time.

Leek & Ham Pie

1⅞ package dry cream of leek soup mix
2 cups milk
1 cup light cream
4 eggs
½ lb. grated Swiss or Monterey Jack cheese
1 tsp. dry mustard
1 tsp. salt
¼ tsp. pepper
two 4½-oz. cans deviled ham
3 tbsp. dry bread crumbs (packaged)
10" pie shell

With wooden spoon, blend soup mix with milk in medium saucepan. Bring to boil over medium heat, stirring constantly. Remove from heat, cool slightly, stir in cream. Refrigerate until cold, about 20 minutes. Preheat oven to 375 degrees. With rotary beater beat eggs with soup mixture. Mix in cheese, salt, pepper, and mustard. Mix crumbs and deviled ham. Spread ham mixture evenly over bottom of pie shell. Pour in filling. Bake 50 minutes until set. Cool slightly. Serves 8. This also makes very good tiny tarts for cocktail parties, if you stir the ham-crumb mixture into the soup mixture and spoon into miniature tart pans. Reduce cooking time according to tart size.

Vidalia Onion Quiche

3 tbsp. butter
½ lb. Vidalia onions, sliced thin
¼ tsp. salt
freshly ground black pepper
½ cup Swiss or Monterey Jack cheese
4 eggs
1½ cups heavy cream or half & half
¼ cup dry white wine
freshly ground black pepper
freshly grated nutmeg

Roll out and line a 9" pie plate with pastry, partially bake. Heat butter, add onions and sauté for 5 minutes until soft; add salt and pepper. Spread onions in pie shell and sprinkle with cheese. Beat eggs, cream, wine, nutmeg, and salt & pepper together and pour over onions and cheese. Bake for 40 minutes at 375 degrees. Serves 8.

Tailgate Essentials

1. A picnic basket (either wicker or canvas). In this, keep packed: paper plates, cups, bowls, eating and serving utensils, plastic drop cloth to cover the ground (if you don't take a table), and a table cover (a quilt, tablecloth, or beach towel) and napkins. Include a bottle opener, corkscrew, and an emergency first-aid kit—a large Ziplock bag can hold adhesive bandages, matches, insect repellent, and spray, and little packets of salt, pepper, and sugar. Include paper towels and a garbage bag for cleanup.

2. A large, wide-mouth Thermos jug is good for carrying hot or cold soups or drinks.

3. Styrofoam chests can be used for hot and cold things. Line one for hot foods with several layers of newspaper and foil. For cold foods, put ice on the bottom and cover with a folded plastic garbage bag, and put chilled foods on top. The ice will stay clean to use in cold drinks and keep the food dry. Also, use a few blue ice packets in with the cold food.

4. Folding chairs.

5. A folding table to serve from. Card tables, folding French café tables, or an old wooden ironing board (which can be found secondhand) are easy to transport.

6. Wicker paper plate holders and inexpensive bamboo trays that can be stacked with eating utensils already wrapped in napkins will facilitate easy serving.

7. Centerpieces and citronella votive candles add a finishing touch.

Soups, Stews,
Sandwiches & Salads

Soups and Stews

Both hot and cold soups may be transported in wide mouth thermos jugs. Remember to take a ladle! For hot soups, preheat the thermos by filling it with hot water, waiting a few minutes, and emptying it.

Cold Soups

Cold Squash Soup

6-8 cups chicken broth (may use reconstituted
  crystals)
16 oz. cream cheese, broken into pieces
1 lg. onion, chopped
2 lbs. squash, washed & sliced

Cook vegetables in chicken broth. Stir in cream cheese. Purée in batches. Add salt & pepper to taste. Chill. If the soup is too thick, thin it with a little milk. For less fat, use Neufchâtel in place of cream cheese.

Vichyssoise

4 cups potatoes, cubed
1 cup celery, sliced
1 cup onion, chopped
2 cups chicken broth
2 cups half & half
3 tbsp. butter
2 tsp. salt
white pepper, to taste

Cook potatoes, onion, celery, and salt in broth until vegetables are tender. Put vegetables and broth mixture through blender or food processor to purée, and pour back into pot. Add remaining ingredients, heating for a few minutes until well-blended. Chill. To garnish vichyssoise with fresh herbs, chop finely 1 tbsp. each of chives, parsley, and tarragon and sprinkle on soup just before serving. (1 tsp. dried herbs equals 1 tbsp. of fresh herbs.)

European Cucumber Vichyssoise

1 cup chopped European cucumber
1/4 cup chopped green onions
2 tbsp. oleo
1 can cream of potato soup
1/2 soup can each: milk, water, sour cream

Sauté cucumber and onions in oleo till tender. Add other ingredients, heat until blended. Put in blender or food processor until blended. Chill. Garnish with a few chopped chives.

Gazpacho

1 cup fresh tomatoes, skinned & chopped
½ cup finely chopped celery
½ cup green pepper
½ cup cucumber
⅓ cup finely chopped spring onions with tops
1 tbsp. each finely chopped chives and parsley
2 cups tomato juice
2 tbsp. raspberry vinegar
salt & pepper to taste
2 tbsp. olive oil
1 tsp. Worcestershire sauce
dash of Tabasco

Whisk oil, vinegar, Worcestershire sauce, Tabasco, salt, pepper, and one clove garlic pressed into tomato juice. Stir in vegetables. This keeps very well in the refrigerator. Serve chilled with croutons or chives top garnish. If you like this soup thicker, purée a slice of bread with the tomato juice.

Chilled Salmon Soup

10 oz. smoked salmon
¾ pt. clam juice or white wine
¾ pt. half & half
1 tbsp. lemon juice
white pepper

Purée salmon & fish stock or white wine. Stir in cream, lemon juice & pepper. Chill. Top with garnish (1 smoked trout or catfish, skinned, boned & flaked and 1 tbsp. chopped chives or spring onion). Serves 4.

Chilled Tomato and Basil Soup

5 cups skinned tomatoes
¼ cup basil leaves
1½ cups chopped onion
¼ cup olive oil
1 tbsp. tomato paste
1 tsp. salt
1 clove garlic, pressed
1 tsp. sugar
3 cups chicken broth

Dip tomatoes in boiling water for a few minutes, then peel off skins & chop. Put tomatoes, onions, ¼ cup olive oil, tomato paste, salt, garlic, and sugar in Dutch oven and simmer, stirring for 20 minutes. Blend 2 tbsp. flour with ½ cup chicken broth, then blend in 2½ more cups of chicken broth, 1 cup water, and ¼ cup basil leaves. Purée in food processor in batches and add salt & white pepper to taste. Chill. Just before serving, whisk in another ¼ cup olive oil.

Strawberry Soup

2 cups unsweetened pineapple juice
¼ cup sugar (optional)
1 pint strawberries, hulled
½ cup claret (or any red wine)
½ cup sour cream

Purée strawberries with 1 cup of pineapple juice and sugar. Whisk in other ingredients and chill well. Garnish with strawberry halves or slices. Serves 6.

Peach Soup

6 ripe peaches
2 cups white wine
½ cup water
3 tbsp. sugar
1 tbsp. lime juice
1 tbsp. orange juice
pinch curry powder
pinch powdered allspice
pinch powdered cloves
sour cream

Peel peaches and dice. Purée in blender or food processor. Put peach purée in saucepan and add water, wine, juices and spices. Bring to boil and simmer, stirring often, 10 minutes. Chill. Serve with a teaspoon of sour cream on top.

Hot Soups and Stews

Cauliflower & Stilton Cream Soup

1 lg. head cauliflower, cut into florets
1 cup water
1 qt. chicken broth
1 cup chopped onion
2 carrots, grated
1 qt. half & half
1 stick butter or oleo
⅔ cups flour
4 oz. cream cheese
4 oz. Stilton cheese

Cook cauliflower in water until tender. Drain and mash. Cook other vegetables in chicken broth until tender. Stir in cauliflower. Add cream and heat until warm but not boiling. Melt butter and stir in the flour. Gradually add to soup to thicken it. Stir in cheeses. If you'd like a totally puréed soup, put all vegetables through food processor before adding cream. Serves 8.

Lucy Carter's Cheesy Ham & Potato Chowder

1½ cups water
2 lg. potatoes (4 cups), cubed
½ cup celery thinly sliced
¼ cup onion, diced
1 tsp. salt
¼ tsp. pepper
¼ cup butter
¼ cup all-purpose flour
2 cups milk
8 oz. (2 cups) sharp Cheddar cheese, shredded
1 cup cooked ham, cubed
4 slices bacon, cooked and crumbled

In a Dutch oven bring water to a boil; add vegetables, salt, and pepper. Cover and simmer 10 minutes or until vegetables are done. Melt butter in a medium saucepan, blend in flour; gradually stir in milk. Cook over medium heat, stirring constantly, until mixture comes to a boil; boil for 1 minute. Add cheese and stir until melted. Slowly stir cheese mixture into vegetables. Add ham and stir well. Garnish with crumbled bacon. Serves 6.

Brunswick Stew

5 lb. hen
2 lb. fresh pork
1 lb. round steak
2 onions, chopped
2 potatoes, chopped
¼ cup cider or wine vinegar
2 cups butter beans—fresh, frozen, or canned
4 cups fresh tomatoes (or two 16-oz. cans)
two 16-oz. cans creamed corn
2 sticks butter
salt & pepper
Worcestershire sauce
hot pepper sauce

Simmer chicken and meat in covered Dutch oven in 1½ qts. salted water for 4 hours or until meat is tender. Remove meats, cool and debone and chop or pull into small pieces. In 2 qts. stock cook onion and potatoes for 30 minutes. Add rest of ingredients and cooked meat. Cover and simmer, stirring often for 2 hours or until mixture is thick. Adjust seasonings. Serve hot.

Chicken Brunswick Stew

1 whole chicken, cut up
1 onion, cut up
2 ribs celery, diced
1 tsp. salt
1/4 tsp. pepper
10-oz. package frozen white shoepeg corn
10-oz. package frozen sm. butter beans
10-oz. package frozen okra
1 lb. canned tomatoes or cubed potatoes
2 potatoes, cubed
1/3 cup catsup
2-3 tbsp. vinegar
1 tbsp. brown sugar
1 tbsp. Worcestershire sauce
1/2 tsp. Tabasco
1/4 tsp. marjoram or thyme
2-3 tbsp. butter

Place chicken in Dutch oven and add enough water to cover well. Add onion, celery, salt, and pepper. Boil until chicken comes off bones easily. Remove chicken to cool and add corn, butter beans, okra, tomatoes, potatoes, catsup, and vinegar; cook 2 hours or until tender. Remove chicken from bones and add to vegetables along with Worcestershire sauce, Tabasco, herb, and butter.

Mild Chili

4 tbsp. bacon drippings or oil
1 sm. chopped onion
1 clove garlic, sliced
1 lb. ground beef
4 cups cooked kidney beans (or two 15-oz. cans)
⅔ cup minced green pepper
1 or 2 cans tomatoes, mashed
2 bay leaves, crushed
4 tsp. sugar
2 tbsp. chili powder
salt and pepper

Brown onion and garlic in drippings and drain. Brown beef, drain again. Add other ingredients and simmer 30 minutes to an hour. Serves 6.

Without the beans, this next chili is great over hot dogs.

Cincinnati Chili

2 lbs. ground beef
1 qt. water
2 med. onions, chopped
two 8-oz. cans tomato sauce
¼ tsp. allspice
½ tsp. red pepper
4 tbsp. chili powder
½ oz. unsweetened chocolate
4 cloves garlic, minced
2 tbsp. vinegar
1 lg. bay leaf, whole
5 whole cloves
2 tsp. Worcestershire sauce
1½ tsp. salt
1 tsp. cinnamon
1 can black beans (optional)

In a 4-qt. saucepan add ground beef to water; stir until beef separates to a fine texture. Boil slowly for half an hour. Add all other ingredients. Stir to blend, bringing to a boil; reduce heat and simmer uncovered for about 3 hours. Last hour, pot may be covered after desired consistency is reached.

Black-Eyed Pea Soup

2 cups black-eyed peas (soak overnight in water and
    drain)
smoked ham hock or white bacon
1 lg. chopped onion
1 clove of garlic, pressed
salt & pepper
water
red wine, sherry, or madeira for flavor

Put peas, smoked ham hock or bacon, garlic, onion, and salt & pepper in
Dutch oven and add 2 qts. water. Cook slowly 3 to 4 hours, until peas are
very tender. Add water as needed (and you will need to add water). Remove
ham. Put peas and some liquid in food processor and purée, then push
purée through a strainer into bowl. Correct seasonings and add red wine to
flavor. If soup is too thick, dilute with water or beef bouillon. This soup
should be the consistency of Vichyssoise. Serves 6. Serve hot with corn
muffins.

Cheesy Corn Muffins

two 7½-oz. boxes Martha White yellow corn
    muffin mix
1¼ cups milk
½ cup oil (or bacon grease with Wesson oil)
3 eggs
1 lg. onion, chopped
4 slices bacon, cooked and crumbled
12-oz. can whole kernel corn, drained
1¼ cups shredded sharp cheddar
1 tsp. salt

Beat eggs. Add oil and milk. Whisk well to combine and stir in corn bread
mix. Combine well and add other ingredients. Mix well and cook in
muffin tins lined with paper muffin liners. Bake 25 minutes at 325
degrees. These muffins do not need butter and are as good cold as hot.

Black Bean Soup

4 cups black beans
smoked ham bone
3 bunches green onions
3 bay leaves
1 tbsp. salt
few shakes hot pepper sauce
2 cloves garlic
4 stalks celery, finely chopped
2 lg. onions, finely chopped
3 tbsp. flour
$\frac{1}{2}$ cup fresh minced parsley
1 can consommé
1 cup madeira wine or dry sherry
1 tbsp. butter

Wash and soak beans overnight. Rinse beans, drain, and put in Dutch oven with 5 qts. water and boil for about 1½ or 2 hours along with hambone, green onions, bay leaves, and garlic. Sauté the chopped onions and celery in the butter until it is soft. Take off heat and stir in parsley and flour. Return to heat and cook 1 minute, stirring constantly. Stir this mixture into beans and simmer 6 more hours, stirring occasionally, and keeping beans just covered with water. Then remove hambone and bay leaf; process beans and liquid in a food processor. Add can of consommé and correct seasoning. At serving time, reheat soup, remove from heat and stir in 1 tbsp. butter and wine. Correct seasonings. Freezes well.

New Orleans Gumbo

6 tbsp. flour
½ cup vegetable oil
2 cloves garlic
1 lg. onion, chopped
½ cup celery, chopped
½ cup bell pepper, chopped
3 lbs. shrimp
1 lb. claw crabmeat
10-oz. package frozen okra
¼ cup fresh parsley, chopped
8-oz. can tomato sauce
3 qts. water
2 bay leaves
pinch thyme
salt
Tabasco sauce
Worcestershire sauce

In a Dutch oven make a roux with flour and oil; add garlic, onion, bell pepper, and celery. Cook until onion is wilted. Add tomato sauce, blend, stir in water, shrimp, crabmeat, parsley, thyme, and bay leaves. Blend well and simmer for 1 hour, stirring occasionally. Add okra and cook another 20 minutes. Season to taste with salt, Tabasco, and Worcestershire sauce.

Black Bean soup, Étouffé, and Gumbo are meant to be served over rice. You could cook the rice in a casserole and wrap in newspaper layers to transport in a styrofoam chest. or just stir some rice in the soup, or just serve these soups without rice. Crusty French <u>bread and butter are good with these soups.</u>

Crawfish or Shrimp Étouffé

8 lbs. crawfish or shrimp
5 onions, finely chopped
2 green onions with tops, chopped
2 cloves garlic, pressed
¾ cup celery, chopped
½ cup fresh parsley, chopped
1 tsp. tomato paste
1 tbsp. flour
2 tbsp. water
salt
Tabasco
Worcestershire sauce

Bring water to a boil in Dutch oven and drop in crawfish (or shrimp). Turn heat off and leave crawfish in hot water for 5 minutes, then drain in colander. Clean and peel crawfish, devein, and save tails. Melt oleo in the Dutch oven (after you wash it) and sauté onions, garlic, celery and tomato paste until onions are transparent (about 5 minutes). Remove pot from heat and add crawfish tails. Put back on medium heat and stir constantly. Season to taste with Tabasco, salt, and Worcestershire sauce. Boil gently about 15 minutes, stirring in flour and water (already made into a paste) to thicken if necessary. Add parsley and serve over rice.

Sandwiches

Always trim crusts off bread before spreading. It saves a lot of filling. The birds love the crusts, so put them outside. One regular sized loaf usually has 20 slices—10 whole sandwiches.

Pepper Pecan Sandwich Spread

1 cup pecans, chopped
1 bell pepper, cleaned and coarsely chopped
1/2 cup sharp cheddar, grated
mayonnaise

Mix all ingredients. These can be spread the night before and stored in air-tight plastic containers.

Pimento Cheese Sandwiches

8 oz. sharp cheddar cheese, grated
4-oz. jar of diced pimentos
3 heaping tbsp. mayonnaise
salt & pepper

Drain jar of pimentos and stir into cheese; add enough mayonnaise to make spreading easy. Spread on bread that has been lightly spread with mayonnaise and cut into halves or thirds. These keep well. Arkansas and Alabama fans can use white cheddar and have sandwiches with school colors.

Stuffed Cucumbers

cucumbers
sandwich filling

Cut cucumbers in 1" lengths. Scoop out seeds leaving a thin base. Stuff with your choice of sandwich filling at picnic site.

Egg Salad Sandwiches

6 eggs, hard boiled and finely chopped
salt & white pepper
few drops lemon juice
mayonnaise

Vary this by adding ¼ cup of any of the following: fresh lemon thyme leaves, finely chopped parsley, chives, watercress, chervil, crumbled cooked bacon, chopped ripe olives. Flavor with a dab of horseradish, onion juice, or Dijon mustard. Make into sandwiches. For onion lovers, try a ring or two of Vidalia onion in sandwich. This can be used also to stuff tomatoes or cherry tomatoes. Chopped shrimp or crabmeat are good added when you stuff tomatoes with it. Also, you might add finely chopped capers and celery.

Mushroom Sandwiches

1 lg. can mushroom stems and pieces
½ onion, grated
parsley, finely chopped (or dried parsley flakes)
mayonnaise
salt & pepper
hot pepper sauce

Drain mushrooms and finely chop. Add parsley, enough mayonnaise to bind together, salt & pepper to taste and a dash of hot pepper sauce or lemon juice if desired.

Ham & Egg or Salmon Loaf

1 loaf French bread
2 sm. bunches parsley, watercress or lemon thyme
    leaves
8 oz. whipped butter
1 sm. onion grated
7½-oz. can red or pink salmon
8 oz. whipped cream cheese

Cut bread in half lengthwise. Scoop out bread, leaving about a 1" thick shell. Put bread that is scooped out through food processor, or crumble to make crumbs and reserve. Remove stems from parsley and chop finely. Mix parsley, onion, butter and half the bread crumbs together and put in half of bread, slightly mounding in center. Mix salmon, cream cheese and other half of bread crumbs and put in other half of bread. Put loaf back together and press firmly so sides go back together. Wrap tightly in French bread bag or foil and refrigerate overnight. Slice thinly with electric knife and arrange in rows. Garnish with parsley, carrot sticks, black olives, and cherry tomatoes in a basket. This can be varied by substituting potted ham for salmon and adding chopped eggs to onion butter mixture.

Seafood Sandwiches

1 cup shrimp, lobster, or crab—boiled and chopped
½ cup cucumber, chopped and patted dry (optional)
3 oz. softened cream cheese
2 tbsp. fresh chives, chopped
1 tsp. lemon juice
salt
dillweed
½ cup mayonnaise

Spread on bread that has had the crust cut off and cut into strips. Or use as cherry tomato stuffers.

Ribbon Sandwiches

pimento cheese spread (or any cream cheese-based
    spread)
whole wheat and white bread

Cut crusts from bread. Spread slice of brown bread with cheese; put white
bread on top; spread cheese; put brown bread on top; spread cheese, etc,
until you have five slices of bread filled. Chill. Then slice into 5 strips.

---

*Cream cheese based sandwich fillings
make fine dips if they are diluted with cream,
sour cream, or extra mayonnaise.*

Asparagus Sandwiches

15-oz. can good asparagus spears
8 oz. cream cheese, softened
½ lemon, juice only
2 finely chopped green onions
dash of Tabasco
salt

Drain asparagus and dry well on dish towels. Mash with fork or purée.
Whisk softened cream cheese with seasonings until light. Whisk in
asparagus (or you could use beater). At this point, finely chopped pecans
could be stirred in, if you like. If mixture is too dry to spread easily, stir in
mayonnaise to soften to spreadable texture. Cut crusts from Pepperidge
Farm very thin brown bread and spread mayonnaise on each slice, then
spread with asparagus mixture. Cut into thirds and store in Tupperware
sandwich box. These keep very well, and this recipe would be enough for
20 or 30 whole sandwiches.

---

*When you're playing Arkansas, cut
sandwich bread with a pig cookie cutter
and spread with any sandwich filling. Biscuits
cut with a pig cutter could be filled with
country ham and mustard.*

Cream Cheese, Olive & Nut Sandwiches

3 oz. cream cheese, softened
2½-oz. can sliced black olives, drained
½ cup slivered almonds or pecans

Whip cream cheese and stir in olives and nuts. Flavor with lemon juice and salt. Stir in enough mayonnaise to make it spreadable. Use Pepperidge Farm whole wheat very thin bread and make into sandwiches.

Bleu Cheese Sandwich Spread

two 8-oz. packages cream cheese
4-oz. package bleu cheese
½ cup chopped nuts
1 tbsp. grated onion
1 tbsp. Worcestershire sauce
½ cup mayonnaise

Soften cream cheese. Add other ingredients except nuts and mix well with electric beater or whisk. Stir in nuts.

Georgia Peach Sandwiches

3-oz. package cream cheese
2 tbsp. brown sugar
3 tbsp. mashed peaches
3 tbsp. toasted pecans, finely chopped
pinch powdered ginger
1½ tsp. lemon juice and grated rind
bread (preferably nutbread)

Blend cream cheese and brown sugar. Add other ingredients and mix well.

Vegetable Sandwiches

2 med. cucumbers (not peeled)
2 green onions
1 green pepper
2 carrots, grated
1 package gelatin, dissolved in 2 tbsp. vegetable
  juice
1 cup mayonnaise

Cut up all ingredients (except gelatin) and purée in food processor. Drain off juice. Heat gelatin in double boiler. Add to purée. Add mayonnaise to vegetables. Salt and pepper to taste. Refrigerate overnight. Spread on thin brown bread. Cut into thirds and store in plastic container. These can be made the night before. Makes 16 whole sandwiches if the crust is cut off before spreading.

Open-Faced Tomato or Cucumber Sandwiches

Because these need to be put together at the last minute, cut bread rounds about the size of the tomatoes or cucumbers you are using with a wine glass or biscuit or hors d'oeuvre cutter and spread one side of each piece with mayonnaise and then put together like a sandwich and store in a Tupperware container (They'll keep well like this for a few hours.). For tomato sandwiches, just slice salad tomatoes or large cherry tomatoes (don't peel). At picnic, put bread mayonnaise side up and put on tomato slices. You could garnish with chopped basil on parsley if you wanted. For cucumber (or squash or radish or any firm vegetable), wash, peel and slice thinly a European cucumber and put in cold water in plastic containers with salt, pepper, and onion rings. Transport to picnic this way and just before serving, pour off water and pat cucumbers dry with dishtowel. Put on bread and serve. Garnish with parsley.

Carry sandwiches already made and cut in square Tupperware boxes with lids.

Many of the meat and fish salads such as chicken salad, ham salad, tuna salad, lobster salad, and shrimp salad make great sandwiches. Chop cooked meat (or drain canned tuna or shrimp), chop well, and add your choice of finely chopped celery, hard-boiled egg, sweet pickle relish, mustard or horseradish to flavor. Bind together with mayonnaise until spreadable, but not runny. The food processor is great for chopping these fillings, which can also be used as <u>open-faced sandwiches.</u>

Roast Beef and French Bread Sandwiches

Eye of Round
pepper
rosemary or garlic
French bread

Rub roast with pepper and rosemary or garlic. Preheat oven to 500 degrees. Put roast in oven and cook 5 minutes for every pound (ex. 2 lb. roast, 10 minutes). Turn oven off but do not open door for 2 hours. Slice roast beef very thinly with electric knife. Serve with sliced French bread and one of the following sauces. *Dijon Sauce for Roast Beef:* ½ cup cream, whipped; ½ mayonnaise; 2 tbsp. Dijon mustard. *Horseradish Sauce:* 1 tsp. horseradish, ½ tsp. Dijon mustard, salt, and 1 cup sour cream.

Sour Cream Biscuits

1 cup sour cream
1 cup melted margarine
2 cups self-rising flour

Combine melted margarine and sour cream. Put 2 cups self-rising flour into large bowl and pour into margarine-sour cream mixture. Stir to mix thoroughly. Fill ungreased mini-muffin tin with 1 heaping tbsp. of batter in each cup. Bake 15 minutes in a preheated 400 degree oven. Cool for about 3 minutes before removing from the pan. These are good hot or cold and don't need butter. These are good with roast beef in them.

<u>Pita Bread Sandwiches</u>: *To fill pitas, lie flat and slit ⅓ way around. At picnic, stuff with filling—vegetable sandwich filling, egg salad, Tabbuli—iceberg lettuce chopped, grated cheddar, bacon bits, and chopped tomato mixed with mayonnaise at picnic site, or any other sandwich filling.*

Traditional Cornish Pasty

½ lb. (1 cup) lard or shortening
1¼ cups boiling water
1 tsp. salt
4½ to 5 cups all-purpose flour
1¾ lbs. boneless beef sirloin or top round steak
4 med. potatoes, peeled and diced
1 lg. onion, finely chopped
1 cup turnip, finely chopped
1 cup carrots, sliced and scraped, or equal amount
   of sliced mushroom
1½ tsp. salt
½ tsp. pepper
butter

In a large bowl, place lard; add boiling water and stir until the lard melts. Add 1 tsp. salt and enough of the flour to form a stiff dough. Gather into a ball; wrap in plastic wrap and refrigerate for at least 1 hour. Meanwhile, cut meat into ¼" cubes. In a large bowl, combine meat with potatoes, onion, turnip, carrots, salt, and pepper. Divide chilled dough into 8 pieces. On lightly floured surface with floured rolling pin, roll 1 dough piece into a 9" circle. Place on a large cookie sheet. Spoon ⅛ of meat mixture (about 1 cup) onto center of dough circle. Top meat with 1½ tsp. butter. Gently pull pastry edge up around meat mixture, pinching firmly together in center to seal. Fold edge over to form a double-thick, ½"-wide seam. Crimp the seam with fingers to form a decorative rope. Repeat to make 8 pastries in all. Heat oven to 350 degrees. Bake pasties 1 to 1¼ hours or until golden. Pie crust mix may be substituted for the pastry.

Pasties

1 lb. sirloin, thinly sliced (or 1 lb. hamburger)
1 onion, thinly sliced
1 lg. potato, thinly sliced and diced
1 carrot, sliced and diced
1 turnip (or 6 mushrooms), sliced and diced
butter
beaten egg
pie crust mix (may need 2 boxes)

Preheat oven to 400 degrees. Make pie crust and roll out ¼" thick and cut into 7" circles using a saucer as a guide. In center of circle, put layer of potato then meat, onion, carrot, turnip (or mushroom), salt & pepper and top with 1½ tsp. of butter. Fold pasty edges up and seal by pinching but leave hole in center for steam to escape, or cut little slits in top. Brush with egg beaten with a little milk and bake on greased baking tin on top oven rack in 350 degree oven and continue cooking for about 30 minutes.

Wrap hot pasties in foil, then in a dishtowel and put in Styrofoam chest to keep warm on the way to the picnic.

Salads

Layered Potato Salad

8 med. red potatoes. scrubbed and boiled
1½ cups mayonnaise
1 cup sour cream
2 tsp. horseradish
1 tsp. salt
½ cup chopped parsley (fresh)
½ cup celery, diced
½ cup green onions, diced
1 lb. bacon, fried, drained, and crumbled

Peel cooled potatoes and cut into thin slices into a bowl. In second bowl mix chopped vegetables. In third bowl mix mayonnaise, sour cream, salt, and horseradish. Into serving bowl (a straight-sided salad bowl is pretty), layer potatoes, vegetable mixture, spread with dressing, then top with crumbled bacon. Continue layering until finished, sealing sides of bowl with dressing. Cover tightly and refrigerate overnight. Just before serving, put parsley sprigs thickly around edge of bowl and garnish with whole or quartered cherry tomatoes.

To give extra flavor to potato salad, marinate potatoes in Italian dressing, then drain well.

Sour Cream Potato Salad

6 med. potatoes, boiled in skins
1½ cups mayonnaise
1 cup sour cream
1½ tsp. celery seed
1½ tsp. horseradish
1 tsp. salt
1 cup fresh parsley, chopped or ½ cup dried parsley
   flakes
1 cup spring onions, chopped
few leaves fresh lemon thyme

Peel cooled potatoes and cut into small pieces. Combine mayonnaise, sour cream, celery seed, horseradish, and salt. Mix parsley and onions. Layer potatoes, onions, parsley, and dressing. Refrigerate overnight. Mix before serving. Put on lettuce leaves in bowl and garnish with tomato wedges and black olives, or with hard-boiled eggs quarters.

Potato Salad Mold

1½ envelopes unflavored gelatin
¼ cup cold water
1 cup hot water
¼ cup lemon juice
2 tbsp. sugar
1 tsp. salt
2½-oz. can sliced olives, drained
2 hard-boiled eggs
1 cup celery, diced
4 cups cooked potatoes, diced
¼ cup green pepper, diced
4-oz. jar chopped pimento
¼ cup green onions, chopped
¼ cup parsley, chopped
2 tsp. salt
1 cup mayonnaise
½ cup heavy cream

Soften gelatin in cold water; dissolve in hot water. Stir in lemon juice, sugar, and 1 tsp. salt. Combine with mayonnaise, cream, and 2 tsp. salt. Mix vegetables together, then fold in dressing. Pour into mold that has been lined with plastic wrap for easy unmolding. Chill until firm. Unmold on lettuce leaves at picnic site. Serves 8.

Lettuce & Stilton Salad

2 oz. Stilton cheese
2 tbsp. olive oil
2 tbsp. white wine vinegar
4 tbsp. sour cream
2 tsp. sugar
1 tsp. Dijon mustard
salt & pepper

Sieve the cheese and whisk with remaining ingredients. Toss with salad greens at last minute in large bowl along with 1 tbsp. chipped chives. This is enough for 1 head of lettuce or equivalent of other greens.

Salade Niçoise

4 med. red potatoes, cooked with 1 tsp. salt, cubed
2 cups cauliflower florets, steamed 8 minutes
1 package frozen green beans, cooked ½ time on
    package (or 1 can, drained)
1 package frozen asparagus pieces steamed until
    tender crisp
¼ cup vegetable oil
½ cup olive oil
⅓ cup diced red pepper, steamed 2 minutes
¼ cup lemon juice
½ tsp. Dijon mustard
salt & pepper
¼ cup sliced black olives, drained
1 tsp. capers, drained
1 can water-packed white tuna

Separately, steam vegetables, rinse in cold water and drain in colander.
Whisk together oil, lemon juice, mustard until smooth. Season with salt
and pepper. Pour dressing over vegetables, toss, and refrigerate at least 4
hours. You may add canned tuna, rinsed and drained, just before serving.
Garnish with tomato wedges, Greek olives, and anchovies.

Cold Curried Potatoes

8 cups potato balls (about 4½ lbs. potatoes, pared,
    scooped with melon baller)
¾ cup finely chopped red onion
1 green pepper, seeded, finely chopped
1 cup mayonnaise
¾ cup sour cream
⅓ cup beef bouillon (1 beef bouillon cube dissolved
    in ⅓ cup boiling water)
1 tbsp. curry powder
salt
freshly ground pepper
½ cup snipped fresh parsley

Cook potato balls in boiling salted water until tender, 5 to 6 minutes; drain; cool. Combine potatoes, onion, and green pepper in large bowl. Mix mayonnaise, sour cream, bouillon and curry powder in small bowl; season to taste with salt and pepper. Pour over potato mixture; toss to coat. Transfer potato mixture to serving bowl; sprinkle with parsley. Refrigerate covered overnight.

Bite-Size Potato Salad

2 dozen tiny potatoes
mayonnaise
sour cream
chopped chives
crumbled bacon
horseradish
lemon juice
chopped parsley

Scrub potatoes and boil until tender. Slice off top and scoop out center with ¼ tsp. measuring spoon or melon baller. Dice the scooped-out potato and mix with mayonnaise and sour cream, chives, and crumbled bacon. You may season with horseradish. hot pepper sauce, parsley, lemon juice, or your choice of seasonings. If you can't get tiny potatoes, then use small or medium ones and slice in half, scoop out center, and proceed.

Vidalia Cole Slaw

1 head green cabbage, finely grated
1 green pepper (cut in rings)
2 med. Vidalia onions, sliced
½ cup sugar
clove of garlic, crushed
1 tsp. dry mustard
2 tsp. sugar
1 tsp. celery seed
1 tbsp. salt
1 cup white vinegar
¾ cup salad oil

In large bowl, make layers of cabbage, green pepper, and onions. Sprinkle ½ cup sugar over top. In saucepan, combine mustard, 2 tsp. sugar, celery seed, salt, vinegar, and oil; mix well. Bring to full boil, stirring. Pour over slaw. Refrigerate, covered, at least 4 hours. To serve, toss salad to mix well. Serves 12.

Creamy Cole Slaw

1 head cabbage, washed, cored & grated
½ cup whipping cream
6 tbsp. sugar
6 tbsp. white wine vinegar
salt & white pepper

Whip cream until fluffy, add sugar, vinegar, salt and pepper. Whip until cream just peaks, but is not stiff. Fold into cabbage. To make pineapple slaw, fold in one small can of drained, crushed pineapple. Serves 12.

Slaw

1 med. cabbage, grated
1 med. onion, grated
1 green or red pepper, finely chopped

Dressing:
1 cup vinegar
¼ cup sugar
½ cup oil
1 tsp. dry mustard
celery seed
ground black pepper & salt

Bring the above to a boil, remove from heat and let cool. Pour over the cabbage mixture and let stand overnight in tightly sealed container.

Fruit in Melon Baskets

watermelon
cantaloupe
honey dew melon
kiwi fruit
red & green grapes
1 fresh pineapple, cut into chunks
1 can lemonade concentrate, undiluted, thawed

Cut watermelon into a basket shape and scoop out red part of melon. With melon baller, cut melons into balls and put into large bowl. Add drained pineapple chunks. Stir in lemonade concentrate and refrigerate until serving time. Pile melon balls into basket and garnish with mint. This is also nice to use as an hors d'oeuvre with picks to spear the balls. *Variation*: Serve the salad in scooped out pineapple halves or in cantaloupe bowls. This salad is also beautiful layered in a glass bowl without the lemonade and garnished around the top with star fruit.

<u>Fruit Kabobs</u>: *Skewer pineapple chunks, grapes, apples, melon balls. Marinate in thawed lemonade concentrate so fruit doesn't turn brown.*

Pasta Pesto Salad

2 qts. florets and julienne-cut fresh vegetables (use
  colorful assortment: broccoli, cauliflower,
  carrots, zucchini, yellow squash, etc.)
1 lb. (8 cups) cooked pasta (*al dente*)
1½ cups Light Pesto Sauce (next recipe)
2 cups peeled and diced Roma tomatoes or cherry
  tomatoes
½ cup (2 oz.) grated Parmesan cheese
8 tsp. pine nuts, toasted in a 350 degree oven 8 to
  10 minutes

Steam vegetables, separately, until crisp and tender. Rinse with cold water
to hold color. Combine cooked vegetables, pasta, and Light Pesto Sauce
and toss thoroughly. Serves 8.

Pesto Sauce

¼ cup pine nuts or pecans, toasted
1 cup basil (or less), stems removed
3 cups spinach, stems removed and deveined
3 garlic cloves
1 cup (4 oz.) grated Parmesan cheese
½ tsp. fresh lemon juice
¼ tsp. salt
¼ tsp. freshly ground black pepper
½ cup olive oil

Combine all ingredients in a food processor. Mix until a smooth paste is
formed. Refrigerate in a tightly covered container, or freeze in containers
of an appropriate size. Makes 1½ cups.

Rice Salad

½ cup sour cream
¼ cup mayonnaise
⅓ cup Italian dressing
salt & pepper
1 sm. onion, grated
1 can drained green beans or 1½ cups frozen
   English peas (steamed 3 min.)
1 package Uncle Ben's original recipe wild & white
   rice mix (cooked, with flavor pack)
⅓ cup cooked & crumbled bacon
1 box cherry tomatoes

Blend together sour cream, mayonnaise, Italian dressing, and grated onion. Toss with cooked rice and peas or beans. Garnish with bacon (just before serving) and cherry tomatoes. Shrimp, chicken, artichokes, or black olives may be added to vary. Serve at room temperature. Serves 8 to 10.

Paella Rice Salad

1 bag Mahatma yellow rice, cooked
4 chicken breasts, skinned and boned
6 tbsp. olive or vegetable oil
1/4 cup white wine
1 1/2 tsp. salt
1 lb. shrimp, peeled and deveined
1 sm. onion, grated
1 garlic clove, crushed
1 cup pitted ripe olives

Sauce:
3/4 cup mayonnaise
1 tbsp. white wine
juice of 1/2 lemon

Cook rice, cool. In skillet, cook chicken in 3 tbsp. oil for about 5 minutes, coating each piece well. Add wine. Sprinkle chicken with salt. Simmer 15 minutes. Turn chicken and add shrimp. Simmer uncovered 10 more minutes until shrimp turns pink. Remove and set aside. In same skillet sauté onion and garlic in remaining oil until tender. Add onion and garlic to rice. Cut chicken into bite-sized pieces. Add shrimp, chicken, and olives to rice. Mix with sauce and chill. Garnish with tomato wedges. Serves 6 to 8.

Cold Vegetable Salad

1 package frozen broccoli
1 package frozen cauliflower
2 packages frozen cut asparagus (or 1 can, drained)
1 box cherry tomatoes
1 can artichokes
1 green pepper, sliced
1 cucumber, sliced thin

Cook frozen vegetables 1/2 time as on package or if using fresh vegetables, just steam 1/2 time. Drain and chill. Add cucumber and green pepper. Vegetables may be varied to suit your taste (Squash is good.). A delicious dressing for this salad follows on the next page.

Dressing:
  ¼ cup onion, finely chopped
  ½ cup half & half
  3 tbsp. lemon juice
  2 tbsp. raspberry vinegar
  1 cup mayonnaise
  salt & pepper
  sprinkle with paprika

Arrange vegetables on a round platter (like wheel spokes) with bowl of dressing in center. Drizzle part of dressing in a circle around center of vegetables in dressing and refrigerate overnight. Carry bacon in baggie and sprinkle on at the last minute. Serve rest of dressing in bowl for guests who would like more.

Tabbuli

  1 cup cracked wheat
  2 cups boiling water
  2 cups tomatoes, peeled & diced
  1 cup finely chopped green onions
  3 tbsp. chopped fresh mint (or 2 tsp. dry mint
    flakes)
  1 cup parsley, finely chopped
  ½ cup olive oil
  ½ cup lemon juice
  2½ tsp. salt
  ¼ tsp. ground black pepper
  2 cucumbers, chopped
  1 green pepper, chopped

Place cracked wheat into large bowl and pour boiling water over it. Allow to sit for at least 1 hour to soak; drain excess water after an hour and add remaining ingredients. Chill and eat as a salad.

Steamed Asparagus with Lemon Sauce

1 lb. thin asparagus, washed and tough ends
    snapped off
salt

Put asparagus in boiling salted water and cook 2 to 5 minutes. Immediately drain and rinse in cold water. Dry in dish towel and place in dish, all tips heading same way.

Lemon Sauce:
⅔ cup mayonnaise
1 tsp. Dijon mustard
salt
1 lemon, juice only

Whisk mayonnaise and mustard in small bowl. Gradually stir in lemon juice and salt to taste. Cover bowl with lid and spoon a little on each serving of asparagus just before eating.

Fresh Asparagus Spears

2 lbs. asparagus spears
4 tbsp. butter
⅓ cup white wine
salt & pepper

Wash, snap off tough stems (they break easily in the right place) and steam 5 minutes or until tender, crisp. Immediately rinse under cold water and store covered until serving. Or wash, etc. and arrange in Pyrex dish in 1 or 2 layers. Sprinkle with salt and pepper; dot with butter. Pour wine over asparagus. Cover tightly with foil and bake at 300 degrees for 25 to 30 minutes. Serve hot or chilled.

Tomato & Basil or Chervil Salad

6 ripe tomatoes, sliced
3 tbsp. olive oil
1 tbsp. wine vinegar
black pepper
¼ cup basil or chervil, finely chopped
onion rings, optional

Arrange tomatoes in dish and sprinkle with herb of your choice. Mix together oil, vinegar, and pepper. Let sit for 30 minutes before serving. Top with onion rings.

Stuffed Tomatoes: *Cut tomato top off and cut into 6 or 8 wedges. Pull apart and stuff with salad filling of your choice.*

Broccoli Salad

1 lg. head broccoli, cut into florets
½ cup white raisins
½ red onion, sliced into rings
⅓ lb. bacon, cooked and crumbled

Dressing:
3 oz. cream cheese
2 tbsp. wine vinegar
2 tbsp. sugar
2 tbsp. olive oil
2 tbsp. Dijon mustard
1 or 2 cloves garlic, pressed
salt & pepper
1 hard-boiled egg

Blend all ingredients well in food processor. Slowly add and process olive oil until dressing thickens. One hour before serving time, mix salad ingredients with dressing and toss. Serves 10.

Turkey & Fruit Salad

½ cup lightly toasted pecans
¼ raspberry vinegar
1 clove garlic, pressed
2 tsp. soy sauce
4 tsp. packed dark brown sugar
1 tsp. curry powder
2 tbsp. vegetable oil
8 cups washed mixed greens, torn in bite-size pieces
2 lg. navel oranges, peeled and segmented
2 med. Granny Smith apples
1 lb. julienne-cut cooked turkey breast
2 tbsp. chopped chives, for garnish

Combine vinegar, garlic, soy sauce, brown sugar, and curry powder, and whisk until well blended. Slowly whisk in oil. Set aside. At last minute, combine greens, oranges, apples, and turkey. Pour dressing over top and gently toss salad until well coated with dressing. Top each serving with nuts and a sprinkle of chopped chives for garnish.

Sheila's Winter Crunch

1 tbsp. cider vinegar
1 tbsp. lemon juice
1 tsp. Dijon or spicy brown mustard
1/2 tsp. salt
1/8 tsp. black pepper
1 clove garlic, pressed
1/3 cup olive oil
3 tbsp. minced parsley
2 bunches radishes (about 12), trimmed, washed &
    sliced
8 oz. mushrooms, trimmed, rinsed & thinly sliced
1/4 jicama or 1 med. white turnip, peeled and thinly
    sliced
6 green onions (with 1" of green) thinly sliced

In a small bowl whisk together the vinegar, lemon juice, mustard, salt, pepper, garlic, and oil. Stir in parsley. At this point, the dressing and prepared vegetables can be stored separately in refrigerator in tightly covered containers up to 12 hours. Put mushrooms, radished jicama and green onions in a medium bowl. Add dressing, toss well, and transfer to salad plates lined with lettuce leaves.

Steak Salad

1/2 cup Italian salad dressing
2 tbsp. capers, drained
2 tsp. Dijon mustard
1 lb. charcoal-broiled steak, thinly sliced
2 ripe tomatoes, chopped
1/2 small red onion, finely sliced
2 hard-boiled eggs

Combine salad dressing, capers, and mustard stirring to blend. Add steak and toss with dressing until well coated. Add tomatoes, onion, and eggs; gently mix. Cover with plastic wrap and chill overnight.

Florida Orange Salad with Spinach

3 tbsp. red wine or raspberry vinegar
1 tbsp. sugar
1 tbsp. fresh orange juice
1/2 tsp. salt
1/2 tsp. celery salt
1/4 tsp. dry mustard
1/3 cup vegetable oil
1 clove garlic, pressed
6 med. naval oranges
6 sliced mushrooms
10 oz. spinach (or leaf lettuce), washed, torn &
   dried in towel
1 sm. purple or Vidalia onion sliced thinly into
   rings
1 cup chopped celery
1/4 cup crumbled crisp bacon

For dressing combine vinegar, sugar, orange juice, salt, mustard and oil in food processor until well blended. Pour into jar and add the garlic clove. Refrigerate. Peel and section oranges, combine greens of choice with celery and onion rings in covered plastic container. Just before serving add orange slices which have been carried in plastic bag or container, remove garlic from dressing, and toss together, garnishing with bacon bits. Serves 8.

For easy crumbled bacon, microwave about 5 to 7 minutes or until well done. Drain on paper towel until just cool. Put in baggie and crumble. If you wait too long, bacon gets soggy and won't crumble.

Mushroom Chicken Salad

1 chicken, cooked, deboned, & cut into bite-sized
    pieces
1 tsp. Dijon mustard
½ lb. mushrooms, sautéed in 3 tbsp. butter
1 cup celery, finely chopped
parsley

Combine chicken, mushrooms, and celery. Add enough mayonnaise to make salad creamy. Stir in mustard; garnish with parsley.

Basic Chicken Salad

5 lb. hen
1 bunch celery
2 cups mayonnaise
½ jar Crosse & Blackwell chow chow pickles
Tabasco

Boil hen with 3 sliced onions and 3 stacks celery with leaves. Cool chicken and cut into bite-sized pieces. Mix all ingredients together and spread top with thin layer of mayonnaise to keep moist (Use 1 cup of celery for each 2 cups of mayonnaise.). For Chicken Asparagus Salad, use basic recipe, but omit relish and Tabasco and flavor mayonnaise with ½ tsp. curry powder and juice of ½ lemon. Serve over 1 lb. fresh asparagus steamed 5 minutes and chilled.

Curried Chicken Salad

3 cups cooked chicken, cut up
11 oz. mandarin oranges, drained (or 2 fresh
    segmented oranges)
8 oz. sliced water chestnuts
1 cup chopped celery
½ cup mayonnaise
2 tsp. lemon juice
2 tsp. soy sauce
1 tsp. curry powder
salt

Mix, chill, and serve on lettuce. You may substitute for oranges 11 oz. of halved green or purple grapes (or pineapple chunks) and 8 oz. sliced toasted slivered almonds to vary this recipe.

Chutney Chicken Salad

8 chicken breast halves
2 cups chopped celery
½ cup green pepper, diced
1 tbsp. lemon juice
¾ cup mayonnaise
¾ cup sour cream
¼ cup chutney
cantaloupe or honey dew melon balls or halved red
    & green grapes

Cook chicken and cut up. Combine sour cream, mayonnaise, chutney, and lemon juice. Toss with chicken. Correct seasonings. Just before serving toss in fruit, which you have taken in plastic bags, and serve on lettuce leaf. Garnish with crumbled bacon or toasted pecans.

Use Your Imagination Layered Salad

8 oz. of salad greens washed, dried, torn into
    bite-sized pieces (use lettuce or spinach or
    combination of lettuces)
hearts of palm, thinly sliced
red or Vidalia onion
1 cup frozen green peas, thawed
1 cup slightly steamed asparagus
1 can chopped artichokes
shredded carrots
thinly sliced onion
sliced bell peppers
sliced mushrooms
1 pint mayonnaise (or ½ sour cream and ½
    mayonnaise)
grated cheddar, Romano, Parmesan (or cheese of
    your choice)

Put greens in bottom of bowl. Add hearts of palm, red or Vidalia onion, green peas, asparagus, artichokes, carrots, onion, bell peppers, mushrooms, or anything you choose. Do about four layers. Spread mayonnaise (or sour cream/ mayonnaise) over top sealing edges. Sprinkle top with grated cheddar, Romano cheese, Parmesan cheese (or cheese of your choice). Garnish with cherry tomatoes, crumbled bacon, sliced hard-boiled eggs, croutons, black or spanish olives, chives, parsley, watercress. Toss well at serving time.

On the Grill

On the Grill

Almost forty years ago (before there were any fast food places or delis) we invited my husband's Shakespeare class over for a cookout. Our dog tipped over the grill and ate the hamburgers. Since that day I have had a horror of holding barbeques. However, my children enjoy grilling and I am passing on recipes of theirs and other friends.

Kelly Mosley's Pineland Smoked Ham

pre-cooked ham

Sauce:
1 pint apple cider vinegar
3 tbsp. Lea & Perrins Sauce
2 sticks oleo, cut into chunks
3 beers
Black pepper, as needed
2 tbsp. lemon juice
1 tsp. garlic salt
1 tbsp. Tabasco salt
salt, as needed

If the bone is in ham, cut a slit lengthwise down beside the bone so smoky flavor can permeate. Soak hickory chips in water for 1 hour and use either electric or charcoal smoker. Build fire and put on hickory chips. Meanwhile, make the sauce by mixing the above ingredients together. Put the sauce in the water pan of the smoker (not on the ham!). Smoke for 2 hours. Kelly says this method is good also to smoke venison and other meats.

Grilled Spareribs

8 lbs. pork spareribs or baby back ribs
¾ cup soy sauce
¾ cup catsup
¼ cup brown sugar
½ cup chicken stock
¼ tsp. celery seed
½ tsp. dry mustard
salt & pepper

Place the ribs in Pyrex dishes large enough to hold them in one layer. Bake at 375 degrees for 15 minutes on each side, a total of 30 minutes. Remove and drain off excess grease. Combine soy sauce, catsup, chicken broth, and brown sugar. Mix well and pour over ribs. Cover and refrigerate overnight. Turn once or twice. When ready to grill, brush marinade off of the ribs and lightly pat dry with paper towels. Reserve the excess marinade to heat and serve as a dipping sauce. Combine celery seed, mustard, salt & pepper. Sprinkle over both sides of the ribs and pat in. Grill about 7 to 10 minutes on each side over medium heat, turning when necessary to avoid burning. Separate into serving pieces and serve. Heat reserved marinade in a small pan. Serve in small bowl for a dipping sauce.

If you wish to cook the ribs at home cook for 1 hour in 350-degree oven, turning ribs and basting with the sauce about every 15 minutes. Wrap in single layer of foil and reheat on grill.

Baby Back Ribs

baby back ribs

Sauce:
2 tbsp. vegetable oil
¼ cup onion, finely chopped
10½-oz. can of tomato sauce
⅓ cup honey or brown sugar
⅓ cup Worcestershire sauce
3 tbsp. red wine vinegar
1 tbsp. Dijon mustard
salt & pepper

Use ¾ lb. ribs per person, cut into serving size portions. Bring water to a boil in a large pot and add ribs. When water returns to a boil, reduce heat and simmer ribs for 5 to 10 minutes. Drain off water and wrap ribs in foil and refrigerate. Make the sauce by mixing above ingredients except onion and oil. Sauté onion in oil. Add sauce and simmer over medium heat. Correct seasonings, cool, and store in plastic container or glass jar until picnic time. Grill at picnic time over low fire for about an hour, turning ribs frequently. Start basting with barbeque sauce last 20 minutes of grilling time.

Orange Spareribs

3 lbs. spareribs, cut into serving size pieces
6 tbsp. Worcestershire
¼ cup onion, chopped
½ cup frozen orange juice concentrate or orange
    marmalade
1 tsp. salt

Brush Worcestershire sauce on ribs and bake at 400 degrees in oven for 40 minutes, turning occasionally. Pour off drippings and reduce heat to 350 degrees. Mix rest of ingredients into a sauce and brush over ribs. Bake 30 minutes more, basting occasionally. Or, if you want to have a smoky flavor, after cooking the first 40 minutes in the oven, finish the spareribs over the grill at the picnic site, basting and turning the ribs until they're done.

Pork Barbeque

5-lb. shoulder roast

Sauce:
    ¾ stick oleo
    ½ cup onion, minced
    1 clove garlic, minced
    ½ cup white vinegar
    2 cups water
    ¼ cup Tabasco
    1 tsp. dry mustard
    2 cups catsup
    ½ cup Worcestershire
    1 tbsp. fresh lemon juice
    ¼ cup brown sugar
    ¼ cup liquid smoke
    pepper

Roast meat in 350-degree oven until well done or cook on grill. Cool, debone, and remove fat. Shred and marinate in the sauce overnight. (To make sauce, sauté onion and garlic in oleo until tender. Add remaining ingredients.) Simmer 30 minutes. Serve on warm buns.

Dr. Wells's Marinade for Turkey, Chicken, Wild Game, or Cornish Hen

    6 oz. plain vinegar
    6 oz. cooking oil
    6 oz. soy sauce
    4 oz. Worcestershire sauce
    ½ tbsp. dry mustard
    2 tbsp. salt
    ½ tbsp. black pepper
    dash cayenne pepper
    5 pods garlic, minced
    4 oz. sweet Vermouth
    2 oz. honey
    2 oz. wine vinegar

Combine ingredients and cook slowly, stirring occasionally, for 30 minutes. Makes 1 quart.

Smoked Turkey

Put Dr. Wells's marinade liberally under skin and in cavity of turkey. Marinate overnight. Smoke turkey in smoker 4 to 5 hours with hickory chips which have been soaked overnight in water put on the coals. Then put turkey in a 350-degree oven and finish cooking (until leg moves easily). Store in a plastic bag in the refrigerator to increase smoky taste. Or if you want to finish smoking the turkey in the smoker it takes about 12 hours.

When we smoke turkeys, we first cook them in the oven until they are nearly done and smoke them one or two hours for the smoky flavor.

Barbequed Chicken

1 lb. butter
1 tbsp. flour
8 limes, juice only
½ bottle Worcestershire
2 tbsp. dry mustard
Tabasco

Melt butter, stir in flour, lime juice, Worcestershire, mustard and Tabasco to taste. Simmer 25 minutes. This is enough for 4 chickens.

To be sure chicken is done through, and to cut down grilling time, you may cook chicken pieces in a 350-degree oven for 20 to 30 minutes before putting on the grill. Brush the sauce on the chicken and grill until juices run clear.

Bleu Cheese Burgers

Season hamburger meat with salt, pepper, and Worcestershire. Make 2 thin patties per person. Between these put 3 tbsp. bleu cheese and seal edges. Wrap a piece of raw bacon around the edge. Cook over a charcoal fire.

Microwave the bacon strips 1 minute before wrapping around the hamburgers.

Tallahassee Baked Beans

Use earthenware beanpot. Line bottom with slices of salt pork or bacon. Then add a thin layer of canned pork and beans, then a layer of bacon, thinly sliced wieners and onion slices (use 1 lg. onion to each beanpot). Add another layer of beans, another wiener, etc. layer and so on to the top. When the pot is filled, pour in a mixture of 1 can condensed tomato soup, 2 tbsp. brown sugar or molasses, 1 tbsp. mustard, salt and pepper. Poke through with spoon. Bake in 350-degree oven for 3½ hours. Remove cover last hour. Put lid back on pot. Wrap in foil and several layers of newspapers and carry in styrofoam chest. This is a great entrée alone, but is also great with any grilled chicken, pork, or beef.

Marinated Vegetable Kabobs

2 lg. cloves garlic, minced
1 tsp. salt
4 tbsp. fresh lemon or lime juice
2 tsp. white wine vinegar
½ cup olive oil
2 lg. onions, cut into ¾" wedges
12 cherry tomatoes, whole
2 zucchini, sliced ¾" thick
2 red peppers, cut into 1" strips
3 ears sweet corn, parboiled and cut into 1½"
  pieces
12 med. mushrooms, whole

For marinade, whisk together garlic, salt, lime juice, vinegar, and oil. Pour into a plastic bag with prepared vegetables. Place in refrigerator overnight, turning several times to coat vegetables. To cook, thread vegetables alternately on skewers and grill over medium heat for 8 to 10 minutes or until tender. Turn vegetables several times while cooking. Serves 6 to 8. Florida's Division of Marketing Test Kitchen.

---

*A variation for the above recipe is to use the
same vegetables, but don't marinate them.
Instead, thread vegetables on skewers and grill
10 to 15 minutes, brushing occasionally with
the following Lemon Butter Sauce.*

Lemon Butter Sauce

1 cup butter, melted
2 lemons, juice and grated yellow rind
½ tsp. salt
1 tsp. dried parsley

Mix ingredients well.

Grilled Corn on the Cob

Soak 8 ears of corn and shucks in salted water for 1 hour. Pull back shucks, remove silk, and wash corn. Melt ½ cup butter, add salt and pepper, and 2 tbsp. of chopped chives. Brush butter on corn and pull shucks back up. Roast on edge of grill 25 to 40 minutes, turning frequently, until done. Or shuck corn, wash, and parboil about 5 minutes on simmer. Put each ear in foil, brush with butter mixture, seal foil and cook on grill until done—about 25 minutes.

Smoked Fish

Smoked fish is a great "do ahead" for picnic food. The following instructions and recipes are reprinted from Florida Seafood and Aquaculture, Bureau of Seafood, 2051 Dirac Drive, Tallahassee, Florida 32310.

Smoked Fish

Mix 1 gallon cold water with 1 cup salt; stir until dissolved. Marinate fish in brine 30 minutes to 1 hour. Soak 1 lb. of hickory or other hardwood chips in 2 qts. of water. Now you are ready to start the fire. Use electric, gas, or charcoal grill with a hood or cover. If charcoal, use fewer briquets than with the average broiling fire. When coals are red, spread evenly over bottom of cooker. They should be sparse. Cover ceramic or charcoal with ⅓ of the wet chips. Wet chips produce smoke and lower the temperature. If available, use oven thermometer with charcoal grill. With gas or electric grill, adjust for desired temperature. Now you are ready to smoke the fish. Drain and dry fish. Measure a generous ¼ cup cooking oil. Keep pastry brush handy. Grease grill well. Place fish on grill, skin side down, about 4 to 6 inches from heat. Baste fish well at beginning and frequently during cooking. Do not let fish dry out. Keep coals covered with plenty of well-soaked chips. Smoke about 1½ hours or until fish flakes easily with a fork.

Excellent smoked fish can be produced on electric, gas, or charcoal grills. Adjust the temperatures according to recipes used. The procedure is the same. Very low temperatures, 150 to 175 degrees, are not absolutely essential in smoked fish cookery. Good results may be accomplished by using higher temperatures up to 300 degrees. Fish takes on a smoky flavor quickly, reducing cooking time. Cooking time varies with weather, intensity of heat, amount of moisture in chips, type of grill, and distance of fish from heat.

Smoked Mullet (or other fish)

6 dressed mullet (1 lb. each*)
1 cup salt
1 gallon water
¼ cup cooking oil

Thaw frozen fish. Remove the head just below the collarbone. Cut along the backbone almost to the tail. The fish should lie flat in one piece. Clean and wash fish. Add salt to water and stir until dissolved. Pour brine over fish, soak 30 minutes, and rinse in cold water and dry fish. To smoke the fish, use a charcoal fire in a barbeque grill with a cover or a hood. Let charcoal fire burn down to a low, even heat. Cover with ⅓ of wet chips**. Wet chips provide smoke. Place fish on a well-greased grill, skin side down, about 4 to 6 inches from the smoking coals. Baste fish well, with oil, at beginning and frequently during cooking. Cover and smoke for 1½ hours or until fish flakes easily when tested with a fork. Add remaining chips as needed to keep the fire smoking. Serves 6.
*Smoked mullet fillets, also; cooking time 40 minutes, or until fish flakes easily when tested with a fork.
**Soak 1 lb. of hickory chips or sawdust in 2 quarts of water overnight.

Smoked fish can be held in the refrigerator at 35 to 40 degrees, with no loss of quality, loosely wrapped for three days. To freeze smoked fish, wrap loosely and allow to cool in refrigerator. Then rewrap in moisture-vapor proof wrapping and place in freezer. Smoked fish can be held up to 3 months in the freezer. To use, remove freezer paper, wrap in aluminum foil and heat for 20 to 30 minutes at 300 degrees.

Smoked Butterfly Shrimp

2 lbs. fresh, in-shell jumbo shrimp
1½ cup buttery-flavor cooking oil
seafood seasoning or seasoned salt

Tartar Sauce:
¼ cup mayonnaise
2 tbsp. sweet pickle relish
dash of lemon juice

Cut shrimp in butterfly fashion by running scissors along top of shrimp cutting through shell. Use sharp knife to cut deep enough through flesh so shrimp will spread open but leave shell attached on the underside. Remove sand vein and wash. Place on grill over low coals and wet hickory chips, shell side down. Brush generously with oil and sprinkle seasonings or salt. Cook at moderately low temperature for 15 minutes, basting once or twice with oil. Turn shrimp over so meat is exposed to heat. Cook 4 to 5 minutes longer. Serve with chilled tartar sauce. Serves 6. Florida Bureau of Seafood.

Grilled Seafood

Oyster Roast

Roasting is cooking uncovered in hot air, and when used as a method for cooking seafood, is usually done outside around a fire or over hot coals. To roast unshucked oysters, wash shells thoroughly. Place oysters on a grill about 4 inches from hot coals. Roast for 10 to 15 minutes or until shells begin to open. Serve in shells with melted margarine or any favorite seafood sauce. Florida Bureau of Seafood.

Grilled Bream

Clean whole bream, score on both sides. Salt and pepper fish. Place onion slices on both sides of fish, wrap in bacon and secure with toothpicks. Grill on both sides until flaky. Florida Bureau of Seafood.

Grilled Salmon with Tarragon Dressing

½ cup Grey Poupon Country Dijon Mustard
½ cup mayonnaise
1 tbsp. chopped parsley (or 1 tsp. dried parsley)
1 tbsp. chopped tarragon (or 1 tsp. dried tarragon)

In small bowl, mix mustard, mayonnaise, parsley and tarragon until blended; set aside. Grill or broil salmon, about 5 to 7 minutes on each side or until fish flakes easily when tested with a fork, turning and brushing with ½ cup mustard mixture frequently. Serve salmon with remaining mustard mixture.

Salmon Fillets

Cover grill with aluminum foil and punch small holes with a fork. Baste both sides of the salmon fillets with an oil or sauce of your choice. Place fillets onto grill over med.-hot coals and cook for 2 to 3 minutes. Turn fillets and cook until fish flakes easily. Do not overcook.

Tuna or Salmon Steaks

Place a ¾" thick tuna or salmon steak onto a hot grill. Baste with oil, lemon butter, or sauce of your choice. Turn steak in 3 to 4 minutes and baste again with sauce. Cook until fish flakes easily. Do not overcook.

Zesty Shrimp

1½ lbs. raw, peeled, and deveined jumbo shrimp,
    fresh or frozen
1 bottle (8 oz.) Zesty Italian dressing
½ tsp. salt
parsley

Thaw shrimp if frozen. In a 2-qt. bowl, combine Italian dressing with salt; add shrimp and refrigerate for 30 minutes, stirring occasionally. Remove shrimp, reserving dressing for basting. Place shrimp in well-greased, hinged wire grills, about 4 inches from moderately hot coals. Cook 4 to 6 minutes and baste with dressing. Turn and cook 6 to 8 minutes longer or until shrimp are tender. Garnish with parsley. Serves 4. Florida Bureau of Seafood.

Backyard Scallops

1 lb. bay or calico scallops, fresh or frozen
¼ cup cooking oil
¼ cup lemon juice
1 tsp. salt
⅛ tsp. hickory liquid smoke
8-oz. package sliced bacon, cut into thirds
    (microwaved 1 minute)
½ cup sesame seeds
parsley (garnish)

Thaw scallops if frozen. Rinse with cold water to remove any shell. In a 2-quart bowl, combine oil with lemon juice, salt and liquid smoke; add scallops. Cover and chill 30 minutes, stirring occasionally. Remove scallops and wrap with a piece of bacon and fasten with a wooden pick. Roll scallops in sesame seeds; place in well-greased hinged wire grills, about 4 inches from moderately hot coals. Cook 2 to 4 minutes or until sesame seeds brown. Turn and cook 2 to 4 more minutes or until scallops are tender. Serves 4. Florida Bureau of Seafood.

The above recipe is also good marinating the scallops in Italian dressing and omitting sesame seeds.

Spiny Lobster Tails

6 spiny lobster tails (8 oz. each), fresh or frozen
¼ cup melted butter or margarine
2 tbsp. lemon juice
½ tsp. salt

Thaw frozen lobster tails. Cut in half lengthwise. Remove swimmerettes and sharp edges. Cut 6 squares of heavy-duty aluminum foil, 12" each. Place each lobster tail on one half of each square of foil. Combine butter, lemon juice, and salt. Baste lobster meat with sauce. Fold other half of foil over lobster tail and seal edges by making double folds in the foil. Place packages, shell side down, about 5" from hot coals. Cook for 20 minutes. Remove lobster tails from the foil. Place lobster tails on grill, flesh side down, and cook for 2 to 3 minutes longer or until lightly browned. Serve with melted butter. Serves 6. Florida Bureau of Seafood.

Kabobs

When fixing kabobs, soak wooden skewers in water 10 minutes before use.

Dowe's Grilled Shrimp Kabobs

Sauce:
⅓ cup soy sauce
1½ tbsp. brown sugar
1½ tbsp. dry sherry
1 lg. clove garlic, pressed
1 tsp. Worcestershire sauce
dash hot pepper sauce
½ tsp. dried ginger powder
bacon slices

Combine sauce ingredients and cook over medium heat a few minutes to blend well. Cool. Peel and devein 1 lb. lg. shrimp, leaving tails on. Cut 8 slices of bacon into thirds (you may precook bacon 2 to 3 minutes in microwave). Wrap ⅓ piece of bacon around each shrimp and secure with wooden toothpick. Marinate in sauce for at least 1 hour. Thread shrimp onto skewers and grill over hot coals for 7 to 10 minutes, until done. These shrimp may also be broiled in the oven.

Elizabeth's Shrimp on the Grill

1 cup plain yogurt
1 lemon, juice only
2 cloves garlic, peeled and pressed
1½ lb. shrimp, peeled, deveined, with tails
1 bunch green onions, cut into 1" pieces
4 tbsp. olive oil
salt and pepper
¼ cup parsley, chopped
1 lemon, sliced

Combine yogurt, lemon juice, and garlic. Add the shrimp and marinate in the refrigerator for 8 hours. Thread onion slices onto 12" bamboo skewers. Brush onion with olive oil and season with salt and pepper. Remove shrimp from the marinade. Pat dry and thread onto skewers. Brush with olive oil and season with salt and pepper. Grill over hot coals or on a cast-iron skillet about 7 minutes, turning once. This recipe is also good with chicken—cut 2 boneless whole chicken breasts into 1" cubes, but cook 10 minutes, or until chicken is browned.

Barbequed Shrimp

2 lbs. headless shrimp
2 cloves garlic, pressed
½ cup soy sauce
½ cup lemon or lime juice
3 tbsp. parsley, finely chopped
2 tsp. dried onion flakes
½ tsp. pepper

Shell and devein shrimp, but leave tails on. Arrange shrimp in shallow 1½ qt. dish. In small bowl, mash garlic with salt. Stir in remaining ingredients. Pour marinade over shrimp and refrigerate for 1 hour. Thread shrimp on skewers. Grill 3 minutes basting with marinade. Turn. Grill 5 minutes more, basting several times. Use any remaining marinade as a dip. Serves 4. Florida Bureau of Seafood.

Smoky Oyster Kabobs

15½-oz. can select oysters
⅓ cup olive oil
2 tbsp. dry Vermouth
1 tsp. parsley, chopped
¼ tsp. marjoram
¼ tsp. thyme
⅛ tsp. pepper
⅛ tsp. garlic salt
1 lg. green pepper, cut into ½" pieces
½ lb. fresh mushrooms
10 slices bacon, cut into thirds

Remove any shells from oysters. Combine oil, Vermouth, parsley, and spices, and mix well. Add oysters, mushrooms, and green pepper to marinade. Cover and refrigerate 1 hour. Wrap piece of bacon around each oyster and thread oysters and vegetables on 4" and 12" skewers. Place all kabobs in well greased ringed wire grill basket. Cook about 4 inches from moderately hot coals for 5 to 7 minutes. Baste with sauce, turn, and cook 5 to 7 minutes longer, until bacon is crisp. This makes 4 servings. Florida Bureau of Seafood.

Franklin's Chicken or Steak Kabobs

breasts of chicken, boneless, skinless, cut into cubes
or steak, cut into cubes
Dale's steak sauce
pepper
garlic salt
tomato wedges
onion wedges
mushrooms
peppers
bacon, cut into cubes

Marinate meat in Dale's sauce and season with pepper and garlic salt. Thread meat and vegetables and bacon onto wooden skewer. Grill 7 minutes, turn, brush with sauce, grill 5 minutes, turn again, brush with sauce, and turn once more for 5 minutes, or until done.

Margarita Pork Kabobs

1 cup lime juice
1 tbsp. sugar
¼ tsp. salt
1 clove garlic, minced
1 lb. pork tenderloin, cut into 1" cubes
1 lg. green pepper, cut into cubes
6 green onions, cut into 1"pieces
½ stick butter, melted
1 tsp. dried parsley flakes

In small bowl combine lime juice, sugar, salt, and garlic. Reserve 2 tsp. marinade. Place remaining marinade in heavy plastic bag, add pork and seal bag. Marinate in refrigerator 30 minutes. In a small bowl combine melted butter, reserved marinade and parsley. On wooden skewers thread pork cubes, pepper, and scallions. Grill or broil 4" from heat source for 15 to 20 minutes, until done, basting with butter mixture during the last 5 minutes.

Chicken Wings

8 chicken wings (or legs)
¼ cup fresh lemon juice
¼ cup fresh lime juice
½ tsp. salt
⅛ tsp. pepper
1 tsp. ginger powder
1 garlic clove, pressed
3 tbsp. parsley
½ tsp. rosemary leaves
1 tsp. dried dill weed
½ tsp. paprika

Oil a 13"-by-9" baking dish. Rinse chicken thoroughly. Mix the juices and pour over the chicken. Mix the herbs and spices together and sprinkle over the chicken. Cover with foil and refrigerate for 2 to 4 hours. Preheat oven to 375 degrees. Bake for 25 minutes; remove foil and bake 20 minutes. Let cool and refrigerate or freeze until ready to pack.

Cold Bacon-Wrapped Chicken

drumsticks and boneless chicken breasts
bacon slices
salt
lemon pepper
paprika

Season chicken with salt, lemon pepper, and paprika; wrap bacon around chicken leg. Cook in 350-degree oven about 30 to 40 minutes until bacon is crispy. Turn chicken after 20 minutes. Cool and serve cold. This is a nice change from fried chicken.

Cold Poached Salmon
with Cucumber Sauce

six 8-oz. salmon steaks
2 qts. water
½ cup white wine
½ lemon, juice and yellow rind
peppercorns
sprig of dill
1 tsp. salt

Put water, wine, lemon juice and rind, peppercorns, dill, and salt into a Dutch oven. Bring to a boil, reduce heat and simmer for 15 minutes. Add salmon to simmering liquid and poach 8 to 12 minutes, until steaks are firm and opaque. Remove from liquid and chill. When I have served this, most people only eat half a steak, so I separate each steak into 2 pieces straight down from the backbone after poaching. Serve with dill or cucumber sauce (recipe following).

Cucumber Sauce

½ cup European cucumber, finely chopped
1 cup mayonnaise
½ cup sour cream
3 tbsp. lemon juice
dash Tabasco
4 tbsp. fresh dill, chopped

Peel and slice cucumbers. Salt the slices and drain in a colander 30 minutes. Pat dry and chop in processor. Pour excess liquid off cucumbers and combine with the rest of the ingredients. Chill several hours. Take in small covered container and let guests serve themselves.

Desserts

Original Nestle Tollhouse Cookies

1 cup plus 2 tbsp. all-purpose flour
½ tsp. baking soda
½ tsp. salt
½ cup (1 stick) butter, softened
½ cup packed brown sugar
⅓ cup granulated sugar
½ tsp. vanilla extract
1 egg
1 cup (6-oz. package) Nestle Tollhouse
    Semi-Sweet Chocolate Morsels
½ cup chopped nuts

Combine flour, baking soda, and salt in small bowl. Beat butter, brown sugar, granulated sugar and vanilla in large mixer bowl. Beat in egg. Gradually beat in flour mixture. Stir in morsels and nuts. Drop by rounded tablespoon onto ungreased baking sheets. Bake in preheated 375-degree oven for 9 to 11 minutes or until golden brown. Let stand for 2 minutes; remove to wire racks to cool completely.

Butterscotch Icebox Cookies

2 sticks good oleo
2 cups light brown sugar, firmly packed
1 cup chopped pecans
3½ cups flour
½ tsp. salt
1 tsp. soda
3 eggs

Stir dry ingredients together and add nuts, cream butter and sugar, add eggs, then nuts and flour. Combine well. Roll in long rolls about 1½" in diameter and store in refrigerator overnight or until baking time. Slice thinly and bake on slightly greased baking sheets in a 375-degree oven. Bake about 6 minutes or until firm and light brown. Remove from pan and cool on wire rack. Take to picnic in cookie tin.

Nola's Ole Miss Gingersnaps

1 cup sugar
2 cups flour
1/2 teaspoon salt
1 teaspoon soda
1 teaspoon cinnamon
1 teaspoon ginger
1/2 teaspoon cloves
3/4 cup oleo
1/4 cup molasses
1 egg, slightly beaten
sugar

Combine 1 cup sugar, flour, salt, soda, and spices. Cut in oleo to resemble coarse crumbs. Stir in molasses and egg. Shape dough into 1" balls and roll in sugar. Place on ungreased cookie sheets and bake at 350 degrees for 10 minutes. Remove from cookie sheets immediately. Nola says that although the originator of this recipe is an Alabama graduate, these cookies have been eaten in the Grove by dozens of family members who are recipients of degrees from Ole Miss.

Peanut Butter Cookies

2 cups sifted flour
3 teaspoons baking powder
1/2 teaspoon salt
1/2 cup butter or oleo
1/2 cup peanut butter
1/2 cup brown sugar, firmly packed
1 1/2 cups granulated sugar
2 eggs, unbeaten
3 tablespoons milk

Sift flour and measure. Add baking powder and salt and sift again. Cream butter thoroughly. Add peanut butter and cream together until smooth. Add sugars gradually, creaming well. Add eggs, beating thoroughly. Add flour mixture, alternating with milk. Chill. Shape into tiny balls and mash crisscrossed with floured fork. Bake in 400-degree oven for 7 to 8 minutes. Makes 6 dozen.

Butterscotch Brownies

¾ cup margarine
2 cups lightly packed light brown sugar
1 cup all-purpose flour
1 tsp. salt
2 large eggs lightly beaten
2 tsp. vanilla extract
1 cup pecans
1 tbsp. powdered sugar

Melt butter. Add sugar. Add flour and salt. Stir until smooth. Remove from heat. Cool 5 minutes. Add eggs, pecans and vanilla extract. Bake in greased 11"x7"x3" oven pan at 350 degrees for 30 minutes. Cool 20 minutes. Cut in 1" squares. Leave in pan until cold. (Makes 2 dozen.)

Chocolate Marshmallow Brownies

1 cup butter
4 eggs
1 cup brown sugar
1 tsp. baking powder
1 cup pecans, chopped
4 oz. unsweetened chocolate
1 cup sugar
1½ cups flour
2 tsp. vanilla
miniature marshmallows

Melt chocolate and butter in double boiler. Beat eggs, add both sugars, and beat again. Sift flour with baking powder and add to egg mixture, stir, then stir in vanilla, nuts, and cooled chocolate mixture. Bake in greased and floured 15"x10"x1" pan in 325-degree oven for 25 to 35 minutes. Remove from oven and immediately sprinkle marshmallows on top. Spread evenly. For frosting melt over hot water 3 oz. unsweetened chocolate, add ½ cup butter, 1 cup sugar, and ⅔ cup evaporated milk. Cook over boiling water until blended. Beat in 1 cup powdered sugar and 1 tsp. vanilla. Pour immediately over brownies and let stand 24 hours.

Never Fail Chewy Brownies

2 eggs
1 1/4 cups sugar
1/2 tsp. vanilla
1/4 tsp. baking powder
3/4 cup pecans, lightly toasted
2 squares chocolate
1/3 cup Wesson oil
1/2 tsp. salt
1/2 cup flour

Beat eggs. Add oil and sugar, combine well. Melt chocolate over low heat in double boiler. Cool slightly and combine with egg mixture. Stir in flour, baking powder, salt, and vanilla and blend well. Stir in nuts. Grease square cake pan and pour in mixture. Bake at 325 degrees for 25 to 30 minutes, or until an inserted toothpick comes out clean.

Reese's Cup Cookies

1 roll refrigerated sugar or peanut butter cookie
    dough
1 box bite-sized Reese's peanut butter cups

Preheat oven according to cookie package directions. Slice roll into 9 sections and quarter each section. Grease miniature muffin tin and press section of dough as for tart shell into each muffin cup. Cook according to directions until slightly brown. Remove from oven and immediately push one small Reese's cup into center of hot cookie. Cool thoroughly before removing from tin. These freeze well. Makes 36 cookies.

Strawberry Tarts

1 box pie crust mix fixed according to directions
    and baked in mini muffin tins
1 pt. strawberries washed and hulled
1 cup red currant jelly
2 tbsp. sugar

Combine sugar and jelly in saucepan and boil until thickened. Fill tart shells with strawberries. Pour over glaze.

Lemon Tarts

½ cup lemon juice
2 cups sugar
1 cup margarine (2 sticks)
4 eggs well beaten
4 dozen miniature tart shells

Combine lemon juice and sugar in the top of a double boiler. Add butter. Heat over simmering water, stirring until butter is nearly melted. Remove from heat and whisk in eggs. Continue cooking about 15 minutes until mixture is thick enough to pile slightly. Strain though strainer while hot. Chill. Put in tart shells baked in mini muffin tins. The shells at can be filled at the picnic or before leaving.

Cherry Tarts

8-oz. package cream cheese
1 egg
½ cup sugar
1 tsp. vanilla
vanilla wafers
cherry pie filling
1 tbsp. Grand Marnier (optional)

Beat cream cheese until fluffy. Add egg, sugar and vanilla. In bottom of cupcake liner, put one vanilla wafer. Top with a spoonful of cream cheese mixture. Repeat until all the mixture is used. Bake at 325 degrees for 14 minutes or until very light. Spoon on prepared cherry pie filling mixed with Grand Marnier. Take to the picnic in the muffin tins covered with foil. Spoon on topping at the picnic site if you like.

Pecan Tarts

1 cup flour
3-oz. package cream cheese
1 stick oleo

Filling:
¾ cup brown sugar
1 tsp. vanilla
¾ cup broken pecans
1 large egg
¼ tsp. salt

Mix cheese and butter. Add flour and chill one hour. Make into 24 balls and pat out in small muffin pans. Fill with pecan mixture. Bake at 350 degrees for 30 minutes. Let cool in pan.

Miniature Cheesecakes

four 3-oz. packages of cream cheese
½ cup sugar
2 eggs
½ tsp. vanilla, lemon, or almond flavoring

Topping:
1 cup sour cream
¼ cup sugar
½ tsp. vanilla, lemon, or almond flavoring
½ tsp. jam (for each cake)

Blend cream cheese with sugar until smooth, adding eggs one at a time. Then add vanilla. Fill teflon coated mini muffin tins ⅔ full and bake at 300 degrees 20 minutes. Cool 10 minutes. Mix topping ingredients. Put 1 tbsp. topping mix on each cake and top with ¼ tsp. jam. Bake 10 more minutes. Transport to picnic in muffin tin covered with plastic wrap. Don't use paper muffin liners in this recipe.

Chocolate Chip Pecan Pie

1/2 cup butter, softened
1 cup sugar
2 eggs
1 tsp. vanilla
1/2 cup plus 1 tbsp. flour
6 oz. semi-sweet chocolate chips
1 cup pecans, coarsely chopped
1 unbaked 9" pie shell
whipped cream, optional

Cream butter and sugar. Beat in eggs and vanilla. Add flour and blend until smooth. Stir in chocolate chips and pecans. Pour into unbaked pie shell. Bake in a preheated 325-degree oven 50 to 60 minutes or until center is set and top is golden. Cool at room temperature at least 1/2 hour before serving. Best served warm or at room temperature. If desired, serve each slice with a dollop of whipped cream. *Florida Department of Agriculture and Consumer Services.*

Carole's Quick Pecan Pie

3 1/4 oz. instant Jello vanilla pudding
1 cup dark corn syrup
3/4 cup (small tin) evaporated milk
1 egg slightly beaten
1 cup chopped pecans
deep dish pie shell

Blend instant pudding with corn syrup. Stir in evaporated milk and egg. Combine well and stir in nuts. Pour into pie shell and bake at 375 degrees about 40 minutes.

Graham Cracker Pralines

24 graham crackers
1 cup butter
1 cup brown sugar
1 cup chopped pecans

Heat oven to 400 degrees. In saucepan, blend butter and sugar and heat to boiling point. Reduce heat and simmer 2 minutes. Add pecans. Put crackers on ungreased cookie sheet. Spread sugar mixture over crackers. Bake 5 minutes and cut in strips while warm. Store in air-tight container.

Peach Bread Pudding

3 eggs
¾ cup sugar
1½ cups milk
2 tsp. vanilla
6 thick slices white bread
2 tbsp. butter
3 to 4 ripe peaches, peeled, pitted, and sliced
2 tbsp. lemon juice

Heat oven to 350 degrees. In a medium bowl, beat the eggs and ½ cup of the sugar until combined. Gradually add the milk, continue beating, then add the vanilla. Tear the bread into large pieces. Melt the butter over medium heat in a skillet and brown the bread until golden. Remove pan from heat and cool. Toss the peaches with remaining sugar and lemon juice. Add the peaches to the bread and pour the egg mixture over it. Bake for 45 minutes in square Pyrex casserole. Carry this in the pan and cut and serve at the picnic. It needs plates and forks. This is also good with blueberries instead of peaches.

American Flag Cake

white cake mix
confectioner's sugar frosting or any white frosting
sliced strawberries
blueberries or canned blueberry filing
star fruit or miniature marshmallows

Following directions on cake mix, bake a sheet cake. Frost with confectioner's sugar frosting. Just before serving, mark off a square for the blue part of the flag and cover with fresh blueberries or spread with the pie filling. Put stripes of sliced strawberries, leaving white icing between. Use either miniature marshmallows or slice of star fruit to indicate stars. (Don't try for accuracy—just indicate!)

Icing:
3/4 cup shortening (Crisco)
2 egg whites
1 tsp. vanilla
16-oz. box confectioner's sugar

In large mixer bowl, cream shortening 5 minutes. Add egg whites and cream well. Add vanilla. By hand, stir in confectioner's sugar.

Menus

French Picnic

Vichyssoise with brie crisps
Salade Niçoise or quiche
Roast beef sandwiches on French rolls
Horseradish sauce
Deviled eggs with caviar
Chilled fresh asparagus with lemon sauce
A selection of cheese served on grape leaves
Champagne crackers
fresh grapes and strawberries
Wine

On the table, use a red and white checked tablecloth and napkins with a row of terra cotta pots planted with red geraniums down the center. Use wicker paper plate holders, and serve from baskets and wicker trays. Serve wine from an ice-filled flowerpot. Send invitations written *en français* like the following:

Un Pique-Nique Français
(A French picnic)

en célébration de
(in celebration of)

la grande rivalité entre
(the great rivalry between)

Auburn et Alabama
(of course, you can reverse the order)

la place: au dehors le stade
(the place: outside the stadium)

la date: samedi, le 19 Novembre 1994
(the date: Saturday 11/19)

l'heure: 11 heure au matin
(the Time: 11 a.m.)

Habillez-vous très casuel!
(Dress casually!)

Richard et Lucie Ricardo
Catherine Deneuve et François Mitterrend
Elizabeth Tailleur et Larry Fortensky
(hosts' names)

Répondez s'il vous plaît par le 5 Novembre
(Please reply by 11/5)

Les numéros de téléphone: 205/678-4567 ou 205/890-2345
(telephone numbers)

(Days of the week: Sunday/Dimanche; Monday/Lundi; Tuesday/Mardi; Wednesday/Mercredi; Thursday/Jeudi; Friday/Vendredi; Saturday/Samedi)
(Months of the year: Janvier; Fevrier;Mars; Avril; Mai; Juin; Juillet; Août; Septembre; Octobre; Novembre; Decembre)

English Picnic

Cauliflower and Stilton Soup
Cornish Pasties
Plowman's sandwiches
A selection of cheeses and chicken and liver patés
on crusty rolls with pickled onions
Cucumber and tomato open-face sandwiches
Lemon curd tarts
Fresh strawberries
Lemonade, cider, and beer

For the centerpiece, use a wicker basket filled with the strawberries for dessert. Use red plates in wicker holders, and red bowls and cups. For invitations, use a watercolor British flag on the front of fold-over notes.

Vegetarian Picnic

Cold squash soup with spinach squares or brie wafers
Rice or potato salad
Egg salad stuffed pitas
stuffed tomatoes
Asparagus nut sandwiches or pepper nut sandwiches
Selection of cookies and brownies
fruit kabobs

For the centerpiece, use vegetables in a wooden dough bowl, a flat wooden box filled with herbs in flower pots, or a big galvanized water can filled with wild flowers. Yellow plates and cups would be pretty with a patchwork quilt to eat on. Put ice and wine in a galvanized water bucket.

Games Away
Listening to the Game on a Boat

Chicken legs wrapped in bacon
Chutney devilled eggs
Tiny new potatoes stuffed with potato salad
Pimento cheese sandwiches
Mushroom sandwiches
Carrot sticks
Praline squares
chocolate chip cookies
icebox cookies

For the centerpiece, use a toy boat, or make zucchini boats by cutting the squash in half, and put in a paper sail on a wooden skewer. The napkins can be folded like sailboats. The invitations can be written on construction paper and folded like a boat.

**INSTRUCTIONS
FOR FOLDING NAPKINS**

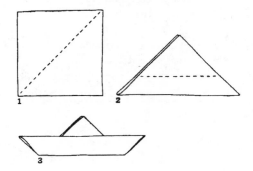

Spring Practice
May Wine Brunch

May bowle
Bloody Marys
Potted shrimp with Melba toast triangles or Oyster Puffs
Salmon loaf sandwiches
Chutney eggs
Quiche of Choice
Fruit salad in melon bowl
Cheesecake
Strawberry tarts

Use clear "crystal" plastic soup bowls, plates, and wine glasses for this one. A damask cloth and big napkins would be pretty. A big May basket filled with flowers will be a good centerpiece. For invitations, write on white-embossed edge correspondence cards.

Summer Football Talk
Fourth of July Picnic

Cucumber vichyssoise
Cold Bacon Chicken Legs
Baked beans
Grilled corn on the cob
Potato salad mold
Slaw
Fruit kabobs (be sure to use star fruit)
American Flag Cake
Mint tea, lemonade, and beer

Use lots of flags at this one: Try red, white, and blue plates and napkins, and a red or blue-striped beach towel for a tablecloth. Fill a white pottery pitcher full of daisies or red poppies with red firecrackers scattered around and sparklers stuck in among the flowers.

New Year's Day Bowl Game
All-Day Picnic

By the TV:
Bloody Marys and beer
Black-Eyed Pea Dip and Frito's
Buffalo wings
Carrot sticks, celery sticks, curry dip

Simmering by the stove:
New Orleans Gumbo, black-eyed pea soup or chili in a hot pot
Artichoke squares, corn muffins,
and butter nearby on a warming tray

On the sideboard:
Smoked salmon
Sliced, smoked ham and turkey
Mustard and mayonnaise
Selection of breads and biscuits
Layered potato salad
Cold vegetable salad or broccoli salad
Mini cheesecakes

Send invitations with a few black-eyed peas dropped in the envelope for good luck (both for the outcome of the game and for the year ahead). The food itself could be enough without a centerpiece if you put the bread in a pretty basket and garnish the meats and salad with lots of parsley, radish roses, and onion mums. Since you are at home, you could use colorful pottery plates and Mexican glasses.